Rabelais and Bakhtin

RABELAIS AND BAKHTIN

Popular Culture in *Gargantua and Pantagruel*

BY RICHARD M. BERRONG

University of Nebraska Press: Lincoln & London

Publication of this book
was aided by a grant
from The Andrew W. Mellon
Foundation.

The paper in this book meets
the guidelines for
permanence and durability
of the Committee on
Production Guidelines for
Book Longevity of the
Council on Library Resources.

Library of Congress
Cataloging-in-Publication Data
Berrong, Richard M., 1951-
Rabelais and Bakhtin.
Includes index.
1. Rabelais, François, ca.
1490-1553? Gargantua et
Pantagruel.   2. Rabelais,
François, ca. 1490-1553? –
Appreciation – Soviet Union.
3. Bakhtin, M. M. (Mikhail
Mikhailovich), 1895-1975.
4. Popular culture in litera-
ture.   I. Title.
PQ1697.P63B47   1986
843'.3   85-21773
ISBN 0-8032-1191-0
(alkaline paper)

Contents

Preface

This book deals with the use of and attitude toward popular culture in the four "authentic" narratives written by François Rabelais during the period 1532–52.[1] In the process, it offers a reexamination of what is arguably the most widely known interpretation of *Gargantua and Pantagruel*, Mikhail Bakhtin's *Rabelais and His World*, a work that itself focuses on popular culture in Rabelais's narratives. Before I begin, however, I would like to present two brief but important prefatory notes.

First (rather than the customary "finally") my acknowledgments. Acknowledging the help—and, in this case, literally the inspiration—I received in preparing this study is very easy. There are no countless hordes of friends, teachers, colleagues, and students too numerous to mention. Many of the ideas at the origin of this study, which is to say my interest in sixteenth-century popular culture, I owe to two individuals: Duane J. Osheim and H. C. Erik Midelfort, professors of history at the University of Virginia. In their summer session class lectures on the Renaissance and Reformation, which they were kind enough to allow me to audit, and especially in the many subsequent conversations I had with them, they made me aware of the fascinating work being done by Early Modern European historians in the field of popular culture and provided me with many suggestions for further reading on the subject. The application of this work to Rabelais's writings is my own doing, but had it not been for Messrs. Osheim and Midelfort, their lectures, and especially those conversations, this book, for lack of its central idea, would not exist in any shape or form. Let the two of them receive here in print the very sincere thanks that I hope I expressed to them in person. In between those two summers in Charlottesville, while teaching back at Case Western Reserve University, I greatly benefited from—and here gratefully acknowledge—the suggestions and direction of my colleague down the hall, Michael Altschul, of the Department of History at CWRU. As with my previous book on Rabelais, Gérard Defaux, of the Department of French of the Johns Hopkins University, was kind enough to read this work in its penultimate stage, providing me with helpful reminders and observations that only someone with his truly vast knowledge of Rabelais and the sixteenth century could offer. This book, and I, benefited in very real and important ways from the guidance of these individuals, and I thank them here very sincerely for their generous giving of both counsel and time.

I would also like to thank Alain Dufour and the Librairie Droz for their gracious permission to reuse material that I had first published with them in volume 18 of the *Etudes Rabelaisiennes*.

Second, a note about the language of this book. All extended quotations from the works of other authors are presented here in English, whatever the original language of the work. In the case of Rabelais's narratives, I have used the translation of J. M. Cohen, modifying it where I preferred a more accurate rendering of the original. In cases where published translations are not available, I have supplied my own. The purists—and I was long one of them—will decry this immediately (I have seen them do so even in the case of so distinguished a Rabelais scholar as M. A. Screech). Here I present my justification.

Though I may be deluding myself, I believe that the potential audience for this study is not limited to Rabelais scholars and students of sixteenth-century French literature in general. Given the approach that it employs, this book may well be of interest to students of other (i.e., non-French) Renaissance literatures, who might find a similar approach to be applicable in their own work. It may also have some appeal to students of Early Modern European history, who are already familiar with the work on sixteenth-century popular culture being done by members of their own discipline. If one is realistic, one must admit that scholars today in both these groups often do not have a sufficient command of French to be able or willing to tackle extended passages in that language—much less as Rabelais used it. If I have translated everything into English, it is to make this book accessible, or at least more tempting, to such readers. I hope, having done so, that they—and the students of Rabelais and sixteenth-century French literature—will not be disappointed with what they can now more easily discover.

Works Cited in the Text

As the old *MLA Style Sheet* so rightly pointed out, note numbers that send the reader to the bottom of the page or the end of the book for nothing more than a page number are more of an interruption than simple references within the body of the text itself. For this reason, and because this study contains many such simple references, page numbers for primary and secondary works often cited are indicated within the text, along with the abbreviations listed below. In the case of primary works quoted from translations, I have followed a dual citation system, with the first page reference indicating the English translation used and the second page reference indicating the original-language edition.

Ariosto, Ludovico. *Orlando furioso*. Trans. Guido Waldman. New York: Oxford University Press, 1974.

———. *Orlando furioso*. Ed. Lanfranco Caretti. Milan: Ricciardi, 1963. Cited by canto, stanza, and line numbers in the text.

Bakhtin, Mikhail. *Problems of Dostoevsky's Poetics*. [Cited as *Dos*.] Ed. and trans. Caryl Emerson. Minneapolis: University of Minnesota Press, 1984.

———. *Rabelais and His World*. [Cited as B.] Trans. Helene Iswolsky. Cambridge: MIT Press, 1968; rpt. Bloomington: Indiana University Press, 1984.

Bercé, Yves-Marie. *Croquants et Nu-Pieds: Les Soulèvements paysans en France du XVIe au XIXe siècle*. Paris: Gallimard, 1974.

Burke, Peter. *Popular Culture in Early Modern Europe*. New York: NYU Press, 1978.

Castiglione, Baldassare. *The Book of the Courtier*. Trans. Charles S. Singleton. New York: Anchor Books, 1959.

———. *Il Libro del Cortigiano*. In *Opere di Castiglione, Della Casa, Cellini*. Ed. Carlo Cordie. Milan: Ricciardi, 1960.

Clark, Katerina, and Michael Holquist. *Mikhail Bakhtin*. [Cited as CH.] Cambridge: Harvard University Press, 1984.

Davis, Natalie Z. *Society and Culture in Early Modern France*. Stanford: Stanford University Press, 1975.

Erasmus, Desiderius. *Colloquies*. Trans. Craig R. Thompson. Chicago: University of Chicago Press, 1965.

———. *Colloquia*. Ed. L. E. Halkin, F. Bierlaire, and R. Hoven. Vol. I-3 in the Amsterdam *Opera Omnia* edition. Amsterdam: North-Holland, 1972.

———. *The Praise of Folly*. Trans. Clarence H. Miller. New Haven: Yale University Press, 1979. This edition contains both the text of *Praise of Folly* and related Erasmian letters.

———. *Moriae Encomium*. [Cited as *ME*.] Ed. Clarence H. Miller. Vol. IV-3 in the Amsterdam *Opera Omnia* edition. Amsterdam: North-Holland, 1979.

———. *Opus Epistolarum*. [Cited as *OE*.] Ed. P. S. Allen. Vol. 2. Oxford: Clarendon Press, 1910.

Ginzburg, Carlo. *The Cheese and the Worms*. Trans. John and Anne Tedeschi. Baltimore: Johns Hopkins University Press, 1980.

Les Grandes et inestimables cronicques du grant et enorme geant Gargantua. . . . [Cited as *Cronicques*.] In *The Tale of Gargantua and King Arthur*. Ed. Huntington Brown. Cambridge: Harvard University Press, 1932.

Knecht, R. J. *Francis I*. Cambridge: Cambridge University Press, 1982.

Moeller, Bernd. *Imperial Cities and the Reformation*. Ed. and trans. H. C. Erik Midelfort and Mark U. Edwards, Jr. Philadelphia: Fortress Press, 1972.

More, Thomas. *Utopia*. Ed. Edward Surtz and J. H. Hexter. Vol. 4 of *The Complete Works of St. Thomas More*. New Haven: Yale University Press, 1965. This edition provides an English translation (by G. C. Richards) opposite the original Latin text.

Muchambled, Robert. *Culture populaire et culture des élites dans la France moderne (XVe–XVIIIe siècles)*. Paris: Flammarion, 1978.

Rabelais, François. *Gargantua and Pantagruel*. Trans. J. M. Co-hen. New York: Penguin, 1978. Cohen based his translation on Jean Plattard's edition of the *Oeuvres* (Paris: Les Belles Lettres, 1929), 5 vols. Unlike those published by Droz (see below), Plattard's texts for *Pantagruel* and *Gargantua* are based on the last revisions of these novels supervised by Rabelais (Lyons, 1542). As a result, Cohen's translation does not always coincide with the Droz editions. I have made alterations in his version where necessary.

————. *Gargantua*. [Cited as *G*.] Ed. M. A. Screech and Ruth Calder. Geneva: Droz, 1970. This text is based upon the first known edition of *Gargantua* (1534/35).

————. *Pantagruel*. [Cited as *P*.] Ed. V. L. Saulnier. Geneva: Droz, 1965. This edition is based on the first known edition of *Pantagruel* (1532).

————. *Quart Livre*. [Cited as *QL*.] Ed. Robert Marichal. Geneva: Droz, 1947.

————. *Tiers Livre*. [Cited as *TL*.] Ed. M. A. Screech. Geneva: Droz, 1964.

PART I

Bakhtin's *Rabelais* and
the Status of Popular Culture
in the Sixteenth Century

Bahktin and Modern Rabelais Criticism

Mikhail Bakhtin's *Rabelais and His World* gives all appearances of being the most widely read, known, and influential study of Rabelais's narratives ever written. Since the Moscow publication of *Tvorchestvo Fransua Rable* in 1965, the work has been translated and printed in English, French, Spanish, Italian, and German,[1] a record that no other study devoted to Rabelais can begin to equal. With few exceptions, almost every critic to have written a book-length analysis of *Gargantua and Pantagruel* since 1968 has felt it necessary, whatever his or her own focus, to make at least passing reference to Bakhtin's study. Michel Beaujour even began his discussion of Rabelais's works by declaring that "Bakhtin's essay throws traditional Rabelais criticism topsy-turvy. . . . Henceforth Rabelais criticism must be devoted either to philological research, clarifying obscure points in the text and uncovering unknown sources . . . or it must attempt to prolong and develop Bakhtin's approach by a reading of the text itself." Indeed, Beaujour maintained that the "only ambition" of his own monograph was to "complete" that of Bakhtin.[2]

The success of Bakhtin's book with students of Rabelais, though significant, pales in comparison with the extent of its favorable reception and influence in realms outside that of Rabelais studies. Bakhtin's notions, especially those of carnivalization and dialogism, have been applied not only to Renaissance writers of other nations (from Thomas Nashe to Shakespeare himself), but even so far afield as to the analysis of contempo-

rary Brazilian cinema. Unlike the works of even the very finest
Rabelais scholars—Lucien Febvre, M. A. Screech, Gérard Defaux—Bakhtin's study of Rabelais has crossed national, chronological, and even generic boundaries, being read and adapted by
students of literatures (and even other arts) that have nothing to
do with France or the sixteenth century.

To attempt to assess (or even to summarize) the influence of
Bakhtin's Rabelais book on criticism in general (both literary
and extraliterary) is completely beyond my competence. Indeed,
as one journal after another devotes an issue to Bakhtin, it becomes increasingly apparent that there are scholars who feel
such an undertaking to be sufficiently extensive and worthwhile
to merit a considerable expenditure of time and effort on their
part.[3] Such a development indicates quite clearly how wide-
reaching Bakhtin's influence has become.

To limit myself strictly to the realm of Rabelais criticism, I
might say that Bakhtin's single greatest contribution to the study
of Rabelais's narratives has been to draw critical attention to—
indeed, to proclaim the vital importance of—what one might
call the "Rabelaisian" aspects of *Gargantua and Pantagruel*.

As every educated speaker of English knows, the adjective
Rabelaisian does not encompass the whole realm of things to be
found between the covers of the narratives written by François
Rabelais. It is used to denote quite specifically one particular
facet of those highly multifaceted works. In the words of the *Oxford English Dictionary* (1910 ed.), *Rabelaisian* means "Pertaining
to, characteristic of, or resembling Rabelais or his writings,
which are distinguished by exuberance of imagination and language, combined with extravagance and coarseness of humour
and satire." Perhaps reflecting the move among lexicographers
from proscriptive to descriptive dictionaries, the more recent
American College Dictionary (1966 ed.) offers: "Rabelaisian: Of,
pertaining to, or suggesting François Rabelais, whose work is
characterized by broad, coarse humor and keen satire." Though
the narratives written by the author from whose name the adjective is derived may indeed display "exuberance of imagination
and language," *Rabelaisian* is generally understood by those
who employ the adjective to mean "coarseness of humour and
satire," "broad, coarse humor," and the like.

Nor has any Rabelais scholar ever denied that there is sufficient "robust coarseness" in the volumes known collectively as
Gargantua and Pantagruel to justify such an understanding of the
adjective. For the first four decades of this century, however
(decades that largely coincide with the first forty years of serious modern Rabelais scholarship), most scholars dealing with
Gargantua and Pantagruel either made no reference to this well-
known (indeed, perhaps best-known) aspect of the works, or
else mentioned it only in passing as a regrettable but forgivable
product of the *gaulois* and Renaissance exuberance of "maître
François," an element that could not be denied but that certainly
did not merit any serious, scholarly attention.

It was Mikhail Bakhtin, with his doctoral dissertion written
during World War II, who was arguably the first to assert that the
"Rabelaisian" aspect of *Gargantua and Pantagruel*, its "broad,
coarse humor," was by no means negligible for someone who
wanted to arrive at an understanding of the author's motives in
writing these narratives. Rabelais borrowed this robust coarseness from folk, or "popular" culture, Bakhtin asserted, and its
use in the narratives was *the* key to what Rabelais's works are
really about, to what Rabelais was trying to say and do in com-
posing his narratives. A few scholars had dealt with the sources
of this "broad, coarse humor" previously, among them Etienne
Gilson and Jean Plattard,[4] but none of them had ever suggested
that it was central to, the very medium of, the author's primary
intent. In a very real sense, Bakhtin added a whole new perspective on Rabelais's works, causing readers and critics to focus
attention on aspects of *Gargantua and Pantagruel* that previously
had generally been either ignored altogether or mentioned only
to be dismissed as unfortunate and not relevant to the author's
central, serious purposes.

It is somewhat difficult to situate Bakhtin's approach historically against the development of Rabelais criticism in the twentieth century, since neither the various translations of Bakhtin
nor, I suspect, the original Russian edition of 1965 indicate what
material dates from the original dissertation, written just before
and during World War II, and what was added or altered subsequently in the coarse of Bakhtin's several attempts to get the
work accepted, first as a dissertation and then as a publishable

book.[5] This difficulty of studying Bakhtin's approach historically is further complicated by the fact that I am unable to determine which works of Western Rabelais criticism Bakhtin had access to, and how soon after their publication.

Given these limitations, it can be pointed out that when Bakhtin apparently first began to work on *Gargantua and Pantagruel*, in the late 1930s, Rabelais was undergoing something of an intellectual devaluation in the critical establishment. The monographs devoted to his works during the final decades of the nineteenth century—which were, by and large, the first book-length studies of *Gargantua and Pantagruel* and its author—had tended to follow the tradition first expressed in print three hundred years before by Pierre de Ronsard, a tradition in which Rabelais figured as a very humorous but not particularly profound or important figure.[6] In 1923, Abel Lefranc did his best to change that. In part of his preface to a new critical edition of *Pantagruel*, entitled "La Pensée secrète de Rabelais," Lefranc declared that Rabelais's first novel was far more than just an amusing narrative; it was, he announced, nothing less than a proclamation of rational atheism.[7]

Lefranc's work, on this and other aspects of Rabelais's novels, has often been derided since—and even, to an extent, in his own day—for its far-fetched interpretive contortions and its disregard of historical context, but the fact remains that, whatever the validity of the means by which he brought it about, Lefranc, with his exposé of Rabelais's "secret," was the first modern literary critic to assert that the author of *Gargantua and Pantagruel* was an important figure in the history of Western thought, a first-rate intellect who had dared to make what was for his time a new and provocative declaration on one of the great topics of human concern.

Unfortunately for *Gargantua and Pantagruel*, the very critic who had brought about almost single-handedly the work's new-found prestige was, to a degree, responsible, however unintentionally, for a subsequent partial eclipse of that glory. On the one hand, the sometimes highly contorted manipulations by which Lefranc turned passages in Rabelais's text into declarations of rational atheism and attacks on Christianity provoked a negative reaction from understandably skeptical readers who found themselves driven by Lefranc's very excesses to almost equally strong denials of Rabelais's atheism, and hence intellectual originality. On the other hand, Lefranc, having successfully asserted Rabelais's significance as a writer, managed to convince other critics to devote to *Gargantua and Pantagruel* the sort of critical endeavor that was a primary part of early twentieth-century literary criticism—a study of the author's sources. The critics who undertook this truly gargantuan task often discovered, to their great dismay, that Rabelais was not the first to express the ideas (on, for example, education) contained in his novels. Indeed, he had often borrowed extensively from the works of his contemporaries. As a consequence, they too became somewhat disillusioned with the claims for the greatness of Rabelais's novels, since they operated in a very Romantic critical framework that equated literary quality to a great extent with originality. All of which is to say that, by the time Bakhtin began his work on Rabelais, critics had once again started to speak of *Gargantua and Pantagruel*'s value as lying primarily in its humor, since the ideas expressed in the narratives had not been especially daring, or new.[8]

In this respect, Bakhtin definitely stood outside the mainstream of Rabelais criticism of about 1940, since he asserted—much like Lefranc, whom he often praises—that Rabelais was in fact both daring (with his almost revolutionary attitude toward the establishment) and original (with his use of popular culture in literature in a way that had not been attempted since Latin antiquity).

Though Bakhtin's work had no effect on Rabelais criticism at that time (it remained unpublished, and largely unknown, until 1965), another writer, also of a very historical bent, did bring about a very marked reevaluation of *Gargantua and Pantagruel*'s intellectual significance precisely at this time. In *The Problem of Unbelief in the Sixteenth Century: The Religion of Rabelais* (1942), Lucien Febvre, one of the great figures in modern historiography, took on Lefranc's assertion of Rabelais's atheism and, using his astounding knowledge of sixteenth-century thought and texts as well as a sense of humor seldom equaled by literary critic or historian, proceeded to demonstrate the very real religious elements in *Gargantua and Pantagruel* and their place in the complex fabric of sixteenth-century religious thought.[9] Once again the literary critical establishment was convinced of the presence of significant intellectual preoccupations in Rabelais's work, however ironic it may be that this conviction was brought about by a refutation of the very work that had previously instilled such a conviction.

While Febvre clearly instigated a major positive reassessment of the intellectual quality of *Gargantua and Pantagruel*, a reassessment that has suffered no relapse or backsliding in the intervening four and a half decades, he also initiated—or, taking Lefranc into account, revived—a critical perspective on Rabelais's works that subsequently became one of the most prominent in Rabelais criticism. Beginning with Febvre in the 1940s and continuing to the present with the important work of M. A. Screech, Alban Krailsheimer, and others, great attention has been focused on the religious thought expressed in *Gargantua and Pantagruel* and the relation of that thought to the theological and ecclesiastical issues of Rabelais's day.

In this respect, by the time Bakhtin published his interpretation of Rabelais in 1965, he once again stood outside the mainstream of contemporary Rabelais criticism. In an era when Rabelais was being situated in the liberal, reforming, but nonetheless establishment trends of Christian thought, Bakhtin presented a Rabelais who not only criticized but also worked to overthrow the established Christian thought (and ecclesiastical hierarchy) of his day—as well as the political power establishment. This time it was not a matter of asserting Rabelais's importance against a steadily declining valuation of that importance. It was, however, very much a question of attributing an antiestablishment stance to Rabelais against a critical trend that was, and remains, very much preoccupied with demonstrating Rabelais's awareness of, concern with, and involvement in the mainstream of sixteenth-century intellectual endeavor. In this way, Bakhtin followed Lefranc, but not Febvre, in asserting *Gargantua and Pantagruel*'s daring, its opposition to the main currents, its alterity. Quite understandably, Bakhtin's work has been particularly popular and influential with those subsequent Rabelais critics who have sought to demonstrate revolutionary, antiestablishment, or at least new attitudes in the novels that Lefranc once described as having been written as "royal propaganda" to support and popularize the policies of Francis I.

Having said this much about the success of Bakhtin's work, its place in, contribution to, and influence on recent Rabelais scholarship, it is certainly time to take a look at the critical essay in question.

Rabelais and Popular Culture, According to Bakhtin

According to Bakhtin, *Gargantua and Pantagruel* is "an encyclopedia of folk culture" (B 58). "In all world literature," he wrote, "there is probably no other work reflecting so fully and deeply all aspects of the life of the marketplace as does Rabelais' novel" (154). Indeed, Bahktin went on to argue, that which was of value in *Gargantua and Pantagruel*, that which was central to them, was a product of Rabelais's interest in the culture of the people. "The exceptional originality of [Rabelais's] work was determined by the ancient folk culture of humor" (473). In fact, "popular sources . . . determined the entire system of [Rabelais's] images and his artistic outlook on the world" (2).

For Bakhtin, popular culture was not simply present in the narratives, or even substantially present. As the last quotation suggests, it was, for Bakhtin, nothing less than the key to *Gargantua and Pantagruel*'s essential significance. If previous critics had found the narratives to be an enigma, it was because they had missed this point and concentrated on other things. "This enigma can be solved only by means of a deep study of Rabelais' popular sources," Bakhtin affirmed (B 3). "Only thanks to this method of research can we discover the true Rabelais" (58). "Up to now," because critics had ignored the use of popular culture in *Gargantua and Pantagruel*, "only that part of [Rabelais's] work was read which was the least important for him and for his contemporaries and which, objectively speaking, was the least essential. Rabelais' exceptional charm, which we all feel, remains unexplained to date."[10] Having studied popular culture, Bakhtin felt that he was able to reveal the essence of Rabelais, "the true Rabelais," for the first time.

But why, one asks, should Rabelais, the son of a relatively

prosperous government official and the personal physician—and perhaps confidant—of two of the most powerful figures in the political establishment, have taken such an interest in the culture of the people? To answer this question—or rather, to comprehend Bakhtin's answer—it is necessary to explain Bakhtin's understanding of "popular culture."

For Bakhtin, the one thing that most clearly divided men into two distinct cultures was their attitude toward laughter. Originally, in some remote and unspecified era, all men had held both the serious and the comic to be sacred: "The serious and the comic aspects of the world and of the deity were equally sacred, equally 'official'" (B 6). Then, at some unnamed time and for some unnamed reason, "all the comic forms were transferred, some earlier and others later, to a nonofficial level." Those at this "nonofficial level," the "people," now had laughter as their exclusive property, and they developed their lives around it until it became the essence of their culture. With the "people" these comic forms "acquired a new meaning, were deepened and rendered more complex, until they became the expression of folk consciousness, of folk culture." Henceforth "official culture," the culture of the power establishment, was serious, dogmatic, fixed. "The official feast asserted all that was stable, unchanging, perennial: the existing hierarchy, the existing religious, political, and moral values, norms, and prohibitions. . . . The tone of the official feast was monolithically serious and . . . the element of laughter was alien to it" (9). Indeed, according to Bakhtin, laughter was "forbidden [during the Middle Ages] in every official sphere of life and ideology" (71). On the other hand, folk culture was now essentially comic. Carnival, the single greatest expression of this culture, was "organized on the basis of laughter" (8). Popular culture was everything that official culture was not: changing, open, unstable, egalitarian. Above all, it was positive, shaped by a view in which death and degradation led to birth and renewal.[11]

If Rabelais became interested in popular culture to the point that he adopted its images and its very world view as the structuring principle of *Gargantua and Pantagruel*, it was, Bakhtin argued, because Rabelais saw just how thoroughly other it had become. So different and distinct was it from official culture that by

using its images and its language, the language of the marketplace, one could step outside the patterns of thought that official
culture had imposed upon its members. In so doing, one could
view the establishment, not as it wanted to be seen, as it made its
members view it through the language and thus the thought patterns that it imposed upon them, but rather, as it really was. By
functioning through and in the language of popular culture,
Rabelais was able to climb outside and objectively observe the
"serious official, ecclesiastical, feudal, and political cult forms
and ceremonials" (B 5). Popular culture provided "an escape
from the usual official way of life" (8).

This is how Bakhtin explains Rabelais's use of popular culture
at the opening of *Rabelais and His World*; it is a means of getting
outside official dogmatism, of escaping from "official lies." If one
follows Bakhtin on this issue through the considerable length of
Rabelais and His World, however, one can see a definite development and progression. Popular culture is initially a means to "get
outside" official culture, to "escape" it, but soon enough it becomes a "support" for the Renaissance in the "struggle against
the official culture of the Middle Ages" (B 274). Popular culture
"was indeed a powerful support for storming the stronghold of
the Gothic age." Even "struggling against" and "storming" are
not enough, however. By the end of *Rabelais and His World*,
Bakhtin asserts that "Rabelais' basic goal [in employing popular
culture] was to destroy the official picture of events" (439). If
Rabelais turned to the language and images of popular culture,
it was not simply to climb outside official culture the better to
observe and understand it. Once he himself had moved outside
the control of official culture, he would not be satisfied until he
had undone this culture's hold on all men and had shattered that
very culture itself.

One does not need to be a student of political philosophy to
see the Marxist framework that informed Bakhtin's interpretation. Marx, of course, had argued that a given dominant culture
such as capitalism imposed its ideology so thoroughly upon
those living under its domination that it became impossible for
these individuals to conceive of any other—and better—way
of life. Hence, revolutionary critique was a necessity. Only by
"throwing off their chains," both economic and intellectual,

could men, the "people," begin to conceive of and then develop a better society.

Bakhtin's innovation was to stress the primacy of language in the formation of men's thoughts. Well before Lacan, he argued that man thinks, can think, only in and through language. The power establishment is therefore able to impose its "official culture" on men by creating a language that reflects and embodies the principles of this culture. As long as men have only this language in which to think, they cannot even conceive of society in a different form. Man is trapped inside the language of his thoughts and cannot observe the ideology of which it is a product and a reflection other than in terms of the forms and values that this ideology has included in its language. Much less, of course, can this "monolingual" man conceive of another ideology than that of the establishment, since he has available to his thinking only the ideological forms that the establishment has embodied in its culture and language.[12]

Herein lay the interest of popular culture for Rabelais, according to Bakhtin. Since popular culture was indeed completely distinct from official culture, it was totally free from the conceptual forms of the latter. By using the images and language of the marketplace, Rabelais was able to throw off the intellectual shackles worn by those who had only the language of official culture at their disposal. He and his readers became able to think in a language other than that created by official culture, and so to see this official culture from the outside, objectively, as it really was. "Languages are philosophies," Bakhtin wrote in summary, "not abstract but concrete, social philosophies, penetrated by a system of values inseparable from living practice and class struggle. . . . The influence of the century-old hidden linguistic dogmatism on human thought . . . is of great importance." Because he took advantage of the "active plurality of language" during his era (the simultaneous presence and availability of both official and popular culture and language), Rabelais was able to acquire "the ability to see [his] own media from the outside, that is, through the eyes of other idioms" (B 471). By making use of "the tradition of popular-festive forms," Rabelais was able to gain a "victory over linguistic dogmatism." "The defeat of this most obstinate and secret element was pos-

sible only through the intense interorientation and mutual clari-
fication of languages" (473).[13]

All of this sounds theoretically very interesting, but it has
little to do with the narratives written during the sixteenth century by François Rabelais. Popular culture does figure in *Gargantua and Pantagruel*, but in a way different from and far more
complex than the one Bakhtin proposed. An awareness of this
use of popular culture will not reveal "the true Rabelais," an essential insight hitherto completely unknown, but it does (I
hope) allow the reader to discover yet one more interesting—
and, I would like to think, significant—facet of *Gargantua and
Pantagruel*. It is for this reason that I take up again, after—and
despite—Bakhtin, the subject of popular culture in Rabelais's
narratives.

The Changing Attitude of the Upper Classes toward
Popular Culture in the Sixteenth Century

Before we can determine the presence, much less the function,
of popular culture in *Gargantua and Pantagruel*, it is obviously
necessary to come to an understanding of exactly what is meant
by "popular culture." For Bakhtin, human society had been divided since time immemorial into two groups: those who consti-
tuted the power establishment and controlled the lives of men,
and those who were subject to this control but did not participate in the decisions of power. (The obvious dichotomies are
all applied: rich/poor, educated/peasant, etc.) "Popular culture,"
for Bakhtin, was quite simply the culture of those outside the
power establishment; it was entirely separate from—scorned
and excluded by—those in power, who had their own "official
culture."

The truth, it would appear, is somewhat different.[14] As historians of the last several decades have discovered, there were indeed two "cultures" in the Middle Ages and early Renaissance,
but their participants were by no means so exclusively segre-
gated as Bakhtin maintained. Current historical research has
made it progressively more apparent that what we term the
"popular" culture of the Middle Ages and early Renaissance was

in fact *every* man's culture—peasant, craftsman, bourgeois, noble. There was, to be sure, a second culture, far more restricted in its membership than the first, a culture derived from arts and books that only the wealthy could afford and only the educated could appreciate. But those who participated in this second culture by no means forsook or scorned the first. If they had access to this second culture, it remained for them exactly that, a second culture (however they may have arranged the two in order of importance or value); they still participated in and felt themselves to be part of the first, universal culture. The ruling class and the educated may well have despised "the masses," but as Peter Burke, the distinguished student of Renaissance popular culture, has written, "The point which needs to be made . . . is that educated people did not yet associate ballads and chap-books and festivals with the common people, precisely because they participated in these forms of culture" (Burke 27). Indeed, as Burke and others have shown, "upper-class participation in popular culture . . . was an important fact of European life, most obvious at festivals." Carnival, in Bakhtin the primary manifestation of what was unique to folk culture, distinct from and even inimical to "official culture," "was for everyone" (24–25). This is obviously a point that cannot be sufficiently stressed in a study such as this. "In 1500 . . . what we now call popular culture was everyone's culture; a second culture for the educated, and the only culture for everyone else" (270).

This situation changed, of course, and as several historians have discovered and shown, it changed quite specifically during the sixteenth century. The learned, the powerful, the "elite," began to alter their relationship to "popular" (i.e., universal) culture during the very period when Rabelais wrote. (Different groups for different reasons, as will be explained later.) Yet the fact remains that because Bakhtin failed to take into account—for whatever reasons—the biculturalism of the learned/powerful/elite at the beginning of the sixteenth century, and then their subsequent cultural shift, much of the very foundation of his analysis is invalid. Unlike so many "New Critics" (structuralists, post-structuralists, deconstructionists) of our own day, and quite consciously unlike the Russian Formalists of his own, Bakhtin repeatedly presented himself as a critic vitally concerned with the historical context of the literary work. (It was for this reason that he found so much more to praise in Lefranc than did his Western contemporaries.) Yet it is precisely Bakhtin's knowledge (or, at least, presentation) of sixteenth-century history, and particularly sixteenth-century social history, that weakens, indeed undermines, his critical theoretical construct. Because he bases his critical methodology in history, without having a sufficient understanding of the history of the particular era in question, the theoretical underpinnings of Bakhtin's study of *Gargantua and Pantagruel* fail to support his analysis. (Just as, I will show later, his failure to perceive—or acknowledge—the "cultural shift" from the first to the later volumes of the *Gargantua and Pantagruel* series largely distances his analysis from the actual texts of the second, third, and fourth books.) Neither early-sixteenth-century French "upper class" culture nor Rabelais's narratives were unchanging monoliths, though Bakhtin presents them both as such, whether to bolster his argument or because he perceived them to be so. Bakhtin's success both as a theorist and as an analyst of (these particular) works of literature is severely undermined by his failure to accord either the sixteenth-century French upper classes or Rabelais's novels any of the dynamism and change that he constantly proclaimed to be the very essence of "eternal" popular culture.

The rejection of "popular" (i.e., universal) culture by the learned, the powerful, the elite, of Rabelais's era is reflected in the change in definition of the very word used to describe the culture in question. As Burke and others have noted, "people" had previously been used to refer to everyone. "Popular culture" (if the term had been in use then) would have designated for speakers and listeners of the Middle Ages and early Renaissance "everyone's culture," a culture shared by all. As the learned, powerful, and elite began to distance themselves from this culture, however, the definition of "people" (and hence of "popular") began to change (was changed by those who wrote and printed and so shaped language). The "people" were now peasants, and perhaps craftsmen as well; they were definitely not nobles, or the learned, those in political power. "The term 'people' . . . was used less often than before to mean 'everyone' . . . and more often to mean 'the common people'" (Burke 270).

Despite the resulting semantic difficulty, "popular culture" is the term almost universally employed by those who write on this topic, modern historians as well as Bakhtin. Such unanimity is far from present concerning the name for the "other" culture, however. The eighteenth-century German poet Johann Herder, one of the first in modern times to take a serious interest in this sphere, used the terms "popular culture" and "learned culture" (*Kultur des Volkes, Kultur der Gelehrten*) (Burke 8). Yet subsequent research has shown that not all of those in power could really be described as "learned" (though this would be less and less true as the power establishment began to pursue education to distinguish itself culturally from those who then became "the people"). Bakhtin used the designations "popular" and "official" culture. Again, the second term is misleading because many of those who participated quite fully in what Bakhtin called "official culture" by no means enjoyed official status or acceptance (think of the many university-educated Reformed ministers, etc.). Power was by no means so monolithic in the Renaissance, or even the Middle Ages, as Bakhtin would have readers believe. Robert Muchambled uses "culture populaire" and "culture des élites"; the plural makes the second culture appear less monolithic, but it can also suggest a disagreeable bias. ("Elite" and "elitism" are neutral terms for very few, and Muchambled is not one of them.) Burke himself occasionally employs "great" and "little tradition," terms which he apparently derived from Robert Redfield's *Little Community and Peasant Society*. To those not familiar with Redfield's work, this disposition of terms may appear rather strange—why refer to the culture shared by everyone as "little" and that held by only a minority as "great"?—and these terms can also suggest an objectionable, if opposite, bias. (I hasten to add that I do not find such a bias to be at work in Burke's book.)

Realizing the importance of having accurate and correct terms for something that is so central to this study, I spent no little time hunting for alternatives but had no real success. As a result, I have decided to stick with Herder's original terms—popular culture and learned culture—and will respectfully ask my reader to remember the complications of "popular" and the limitations of "learned" as he or she proceeds through this study.

And now, to *Gargantua and Pantagruel* itself.

PART II

Rabelais and Popular Culture

1

The Presence and Exclusion of Popular Culture in *Pantagruel* and *Gargantua*

We start with the first of Rabelais's fictional narratives, *Pantagruel* (1532). Contrary to Bakhtin's assertion, popular culture is not *the* dominant voice here, though it is certainly very important, and on an almost equal footing with learned culture. In the very first chapter, while recounting the effects of the great medlars on those who ate them, Alcofribas Nasier, the narrator, mentions "some [who] swelled in the belly. . . . Their bellies became round, like great tuns, whence comes the written phrase *ventrem omnipotentem*" (172; *P* 11). Learned culture: a Latin phrase, reference to a written text.[1] "Others grew in the length of that member which is called Nature's labourer. . . . Of these the stock is extinct, so the women say. For they are continually lamenting that

> There are no more of those stout, &c.

You know the rest of the song" (172; *P* 11–12). Popular culture: a popular song, cited to support one of the narrator's statements (and, in support of Burke's assertion concerning the universality of popular culture, the narrator's aside to his generally learned, "establishment" readers: "You know the rest of the song.").

There are many examples of the equal importance accorded popular and learned culture in *Pantagruel*. Developing a comparison to describe the bizarre occurrences at Pantagruel's birth, Nasier recounts the story of how Phaeton "scorch[ed] a large portion of the sky." This heavenly part "the Philosophers call *Via lactea*, and simpletons call St. James's Path" (175; *P* 18). Just before Pantagruel is born "great drops of water were plainly seen to break out of the earth, as when someone bursts into a copious sweat. . . . Some said that there was not a drop of moisture in the air from which they could expect rain, and that the earth was making up for this lack. Other learned people said that it was rain from the Antipodes, about which Seneca tells in the fourth book of his *Questiones naturales*, in speaking of the origin and source of the River Nile" (176; *P* 19). When Badebec, Pantagruel's mother, dies in childbirth, Gargantua "on either side . . . found sophistical arguments which took his breath away. For he framed them very well *in modo et figura*" (177; *P* 20–21). Within moments, however, this student of sophistic dialectic takes off his coat so that he can put on his jacket "the better to entertain the women who have been in attendance on Badebec [*les commères*]" (178; *P* 21). After Pantagruel demonstrates his own skill in disputation, "all the world began to be loud with talk of his amazing knowledge, even to the elderly laundresses, go-betweens, roast-meat sellers, penknife-merchants, and others, who called out 'That's he!' when he passed through the streets. At this he was as delighted as Demosthenes, the prince of Greek orators, when a bent old woman pointed her finger at him and said: 'That is the man!'" (202; *P* 56). When the Dipsodians awake and find their camp flooded, "some said that it was the end of the world and the last judgment, which is to be consummated by fire; others that the gods of the sea—Neptune and the others—were attacking them, and that in fact it was salt and sea-water" (260; *P* 150). These six examples—to which more could be added—indicate clearly that popular culture is treated in much the same way as learned culture in *Pantagruel*, and with more or less the same frequency. The narrator cites "simpletons" like "philosophers," "elderly laundresses" along with Demosthenes. Though Gargantua has studied sophistic logic, he still feels comfortable going out to celebrate with *les commères*. Indeed—and not surprisingly—Nasier himself moves in both cultures and makes no attempt to disguise the fact. He certainly participates in learned culture: for example, he is a student of the classics, someone who is always talking about writing books. For that matter, he is a member of the inner circle of the Prince of Utopie. Yet his origin, and his way of describing it, is "popular." He writes *Pantagruel* when "by [Pantagruel's] leave I have come to visit my neck of the woods [*mon pays de vache*], and discover if any of my kindred survives there" (168; *P* 7).

Pantagruel was certainly written for participants in learned, establishment culture. But popular culture is definitely as "respected" in it as its city cousin. The narrator turns as often to one as to the other to make his points and by repeatedly doing so seems to suggest an assurance that a similar attitude was held by his readers. In citing examples of popular culture, Nasier and his creator seem to imply that they spoke to and operated in a world that did not know Bakhtin's cultural segregation. Participants in learned culture in 1532—at least as Nasier and Rabelais saw them—may well have preferred learned culture to popular culture, esteeming the former to be nobler, more profound, or whatever. But as the examples cited show, these participants did not forsake or forget popular culture: "You know the rest of the song."

Within the two or three years that separate *Gargantua* from *Pantagruel*[2] a great deal changed, at least for Rabelais, and perhaps for his readers, at least as he perceived them. Bakhtin may well have misrepresented the role of popular culture in *Pantagruel* by refusing to acknowledge the equal presence and significance of learned culture in the text, but he was certainly correct in claiming that popular culture played an important part in Rabelais's first narrative. It is with *Gargantua* that his notion of Rabelais's "essence" really begins to distance him from the text, however, actually blinding him to what is happening on the pages of the novel. For in *Gargantua*, though Bakhtin seems never to have noticed it, there begins a systematic and radical exclusion of popular culture.

It starts at the very beginning, in the Prologue itself. Developing an extended explanation of how readers should approach his new book, Nasier borrows a story about Alcibiades and Socrates from "that dialogue of Plato's entitled *The Symposium*" (37; *G* 9). More classical references follow: "Plato . . . in the second book of his *Republic*" (38; *G* 13); "Galen . . . in his third Book, *On the Natural Faculties*, and in his eleventh, *On the Parts of the Body and their Functions*" (38; *G* 14); Homer, Plutarch, Heraclides Ponticus, Eustatius, Phornutius, Politian (38; *G* 15); Ovid's *Metamorphoses* (38; *G* 16); Ennius and Horace (39; *G* 17); Demosthenes and his *Orations* (39; *G* 18). But of examples from popular culture, not a one.

To substantiate his declaration that Gargamelle was pregnant with Gargantua for eleven months, Nasier cites Homer, Aulus Gellius (third book), Hippocrates (*lib. De alimento*), and six other classical authors, as well as a host of Latin legal texts (46–47; *G* 32–35). From popular culture, nothing. In support of his claims concerning Gargantua's birth, the narrator turns to classical mythology and Pliny (53; *G* 51–52), but not to popular culture. The *commères* and midwives who were in attendance on Badebec in *Pantagruel* have disappeared, being replaced by "company" (Fr. *assistans*) who are educated enough to be familiar with "ancient Hebrew customs" (53; *G* 53). When discussing the proper procedure for attaching one's vest to one's britches, Nasier cites "Ockham in [his criticism of] the *Expositions* of Master Breechesman" (55; *G* 57).[3] When arguing the meaning of white and blue, the narrator mentions ancient Thracians and Cretians, Laurentius Valla, Pericles, Alexander of Aphrodisias, Proclus, Xenophon, Galen, and a host of other classical authors (60–61; *G* 70–77), promising to write a book on the subject in which he will prove his point "both by philosophical arguments and by accepted authorities, approved by the whole ancient world" (59; *G* 69). And on and on.[4]

Bakhtin indicates no difference between *Pantagruel* and Rabelais's subsequent novels in the use of popular culture. Yet as these examples make abundantly clear, and as even as examination of the relative frequency of Bakhtin's own citations from *Pantagruel* and the later novels might suggest, beginning with *Gargantua* popular culture definitely loses the equal footing with learned culture that it had enjoyed in *Pantagruel*.

One of the best examples of this progressive devaluation and exclusion is a change that occurs, not between the first and second narratives, but within the text of *Gargantua* itself. Chapter 22 contains a list of the games that young Gargantua played before being tutored by Ponocrates (83–85; *G* 134–40). If anything in the novel, or even in *Gargantua and Pantagruel* as a whole, qualifies Rabelais's text as an "encyclopedia of folk culture" (B 58), this is certainly it. As Michel Psichari demonstrated years ago after a considerable amount of historical investigation,[5] the 145 pastimes of the original 1534–35 edition (217 by

Rabelais's final, 1542 revision) comprise a veritable catalogue of games that were current during the sixteenth century—current, it would seem, with just about anyone who played games.

Once under Ponocrates' tutelage, Gargantua still plays games, but of a different type—or cultural affiliation. When it rained, Gargantua and his mentor "revived the ancient game of Greek dice, as described by Leonicus. . . . While they played this game they recalled to mind those passages from ancient authors in which mention is made of it, or some metaphor drawn from it" (92; G 156). Popular culture is here excluded from the world of learning and power before the reader's very eyes.

A scene which parallels and perhaps presages this one is that describing the young giant's discovery of the perfect arse-wipe.

Bakhtin spent many pages in *Rabelais and His World* arguing that "scatological obscenity" was an essential manifestation of "the tradition of folk culture in Rabelais' work" (B 109 et passim). As readers of Bakhtin know, excrement is an important facet of what Bakhtin called the "material bodily lower stratum," which, in turn, Bakhtin felt to be "the organizing principle of the entire system of Rabelaisian images" (B 126). According to Bakhtin, Rabelais made use of this aspect of popular culture because it was completely rejected and denied by the serious "official culture" that (Bakhtin's) Rabelais was trying to escape (or assail, or destroy): the "bodily element opposes the serious medieval world of fear and oppression with all its intimidating and intimidated ideology" (B 226).

According to Bakhtin, excrement was "ambivalent" in popular culture:

The slinging of excrement and drenching in urine are traditional debasing gestures. . . . [They] are based on a literal debasement in terms of topography of the body, that is, a reference to the bodily lower stratum, the zone of the genital organs. This signifies destruction, a grave for the one who is debased. But such debasing gestures and expressions are ambivalent since the lower stratum is not only a bodily grave but also the area of the genital organs, the fertilizing and generating stratum. Therefore, in the images of urine and excrement is preserved the essential link with birth, fertility, renewal, welfare. [B 148]

If official culture condemned anything having to do with the "material bodily lower stratum," such as excrement, this was not simply because it rejected the unclean and its associated degradation, but also because (according to Bakhtin) official culture could not tolerate this ambivalence, which it perceived to be a threat to its own closed, fixed ideology and presentation of the world.

Bakhtin's notion of the ambivalence of popular-culture images, and especially of Rabelais's use of the material bodily lower stratum, is one of the features of *Rabelais and His World* that has most interested Bakhtin's non-*seiziémiste* readers, which is rather ironic because it is one of the aspects of Bakhtin that is most open to historical criticism. As students of Renaissance history and culture are quick—and quite right—to point out, excremental imagery was by no means so rejected by or absent from "official culture" as Bakhtin repeatedly insisted. As Peter Burke mentions (70), and as Alban J. Krailsheimer has demonstrated with extensive documentation, images of the excremental figured prominently in the discourse of at least one official, establishment group with which Rabelais himself had had very close contact: the Franciscans.[6] Indeed, as Krailsheimer has shown, Franciscan preachers such as Olivier Maillard filled their sermons with scatological imagery so abundantly and unrestrainedly as to make even Rabelais seem mild by comparison.

Though references to the "material bodily lower stratum" were by no means so shunned, or feared, by the power establishment as Bakhtin asserted—with almost no historical documentation, it might be added—it is nonetheless true that excrement did figure far more prominently in popular culture than in its learned cousin. As Robert Muchambled phrases it, "Peasant culture attributed importance to the lower half of the human body" (118). Although the "ambivalence" of excrement in popular culture still strikes me as questionable—again, Bakhtin substituted constant affirmation for historical documentation—no modern historian would deny that the fecal portion of the material bodily lower stratum figured prominently in many aspects of medieval and Renaissance popular culture.

Nor would anyone deny that the scatological figures prominently in *Pantagruel*. Indeed, it may strike some readers as unnecessary and even suspect if I insist—as I do—on enumerating some of its more marked manifestations. (I will be brief.) When

Pantagruel throttles the student from Limoges in order to stop him from speaking his pretentiously Latinized French and "pursuade" him to speak "naturally," "the poor Limousin beshat all his breeches" (185; *P* 34). When, after having considered the dispute of Kissmyarse [Baisecul] and Suckfizzle [Humevesne] for forty-six weeks, the legal authorities summoned by the king are still not able to understand the case, "they most villainously beshat themselves for shame" (203; *P* 57). When the great English savant Thaumaste begins to feel himself bested by Panurge in their debate, "[he] got up in great alarm, but as he did so let a great baker's fart—for the bran followed it—and stank like all the devils. Upon which the spectators began to hold their noses, since he was shitting himself with anguish" (236; *P* 111). While celebrating his destruction of 659 Dipsodian cavalrymen, Panurge becomes so excited that

he gave a fart, a leap, and a whistle, and joyously cried aloud: "Long live Pantagruel!" At this sight, Pantagruel tried to do the same. But with the fart he blew, he engendered more than fifty-three thousand little men, misshapen dwarfs; and with a poop, which he made, he engendered as many little bowed women, such as you see in various places, and who never grow, except downwards like cows' tails, or in circumference, like Limousin turnips. . . . [Pantagruel] called them pygmies. . . . These little stumps of men . . . most readily lose their tempers; the physical reason for which is that they have their heart close to their shit. [255–56; *P* 143]

While sprinkling salt in the open mouths of the sleeping Dipsodian army, "Pantagruel felt a desire to piss; and he pissed over the [Dipsodian] camp, so well and copiously that he drowned them all, and there was a special flood for thirty miles round" (259; *P* 149). When Carpalim makes a move to help Pantagruel in the latter's fight with Werewolf (Loupgarou), "a giant said to him: 'By Gobbler, the nephew of Mahoun, if you stir from here I'll shove you up the bottom of my breeches, like a suppository'" (263; *P* 156).[7] Among others seen by Epistemon during his sojourn in Hell are François Villon and Xerxes, the latter reduced to the position of a mustard peddler. When Villon found that Xerxes charged too much for his mustard, he "pissed into his tub, as mustard-makers do in Paris" (269; *P* 165). After Panurge reattaches Epistemon's severed head, the pedagogue "began to breathe, then to open his eyes, then to yawn, and then he blew a great household fart" (265; *P* 159). The hot sulphur springs at Couterets, Limons, Dax, Balarne, Neris, Bourbon-Lancy, and elsewhere are explained as a result of the fact that one day Pantagruel "was taken with a hot-piss, which pained him more than you might imagine. But his doctors came to his aid, and most successfully. For with plenty of lenitive and diuretic drugs they made him piss his complaint away" (275; *P* 174).

Two episodes are particularly notable. To get revenge on a "great Parisian lady" (*une haulte dame de Paris*) who rejected his advances, Panurge sprinkles her expensive garments with the pulverized genitalia of a bitch in heat. As a result, every dog in Paris tries to mount the woman when she walks (and soon runs) home from church: "Smelling her and pissing all over her . . . these beastly dogs shat all over her and pissed over all her clothes." "A great greyhound wet . . . her on the head . . . and the little ones pissed on her shoes. . . . Everywhere she passed fresh hosts of dogs followed her trail, pissing in the road where her gown had touched it. . . . The dogs ran up from two miles around and pissed so hard against the gate of the house, that they made a stream with their urine big enough for the ducks to swim in" (244; *P* 124–25). Pantagruel "went to see the show, which he found very fine and original" (244; *P* 124). Indeed, Pantagruel is remarkably unoffended by excrement. When Alcofribas Nasier finally emerges from "the world in Pantagruel's mouth," the young giant asks "Where did you shit?" "In your throat, my lord," Nasier replies, to which Pantagruel responds: "Ha, ha. You're a fine fellow. . . . I confer on you the Wardenship of Salmigundin" (275; *P* 174).

It is very difficult to find evidence for Bakhtin's assertion that excrement is ambivalent in *Pantagruel*. Contact with it certainly degrades the Parisian lady, but there is no indication that it "renews" her. (Nor does there seem to be any "renewal" for the student from Limoges, Thaumaste, or Xerxes.) Excrement does not seem either to degrade or to renew Pantagruel. But as Pantagruel's reactions to the affair of the great Parisian lady and Alcofribas Nasier's frankness indicate, excrement is accepted in *Pantagruel* as a part of life—indeed, even as a sign of life, in the case of Epistemon's revival—as it was in popular culture.

In *Pantagruel*, but certainly not in *Gargantua*, or at least not after chapter 14. Rabelais's second novel starts off every bit as open to fecal matter as the first. Gargamelle goes into labor with Gargantua as a result of having eaten too many tainted tripes, which, as the narrator reminds us, amounted to so much "fine fecal matter" (48; *G* 37, 38). Young Gargantua certainly produces continual reminders of these origins: "He shat himself every hour. For he was amazingly phlegmatic in his bowel movements" (54; *G* 55); "he pissed in his shoes, shat in his shirt, snivelled into his soup, and paddled about everywhere" (62; *G* 79). And his conversation, not surprisingly, is as full of fecal matter as his britches. Having led his father's guests to his room to see his "stable," young Gargantua asks them:

> "Would you like an Obbly-oy [*une aubelière*]?"
> "What's that?" they asked.
> "Oh, that's five turds to make yourself a muzzle." [65; *G* 85]

When the poor guests miss one of the young giant's conundrums, he suggests that "they [make] your nose into a tap to draw off a measure of dung, and your throat into a funnel to pour it into another vessel, because the bottom of that one was out." No hesitancy about including excrement here, in word or deed.

Then one day when Gargantua is five, his father returns from a distant war and, checking in on his son, asks the child's governesses "whether they had kept him sweet [*blanc*] and clean" (66; *G* 88). The young lad himself quickly responds that "he had taken these precautions himself, and that there was not a cleaner boy in all the land."

> "How did you do that?" asked Grandgousier.
> "By long and curious experiments," replied Gargantua. "I have invented a method of wiping my arse which is most lordly, the most excellent, and the most convenient that ever was seen."

Gargantua spends the rest of the chapter recounting his many experiments with a variety of novel arse-wipes. Grandgousier's conclusion: "What a good head you've got [*tu as bon sens*], my little fellow! . . . You have more sense than your years [*tu as de raison plus que d'aage*]" (68; *G* 92). Indeed, Grandgousier was "beside himself with admiration, as he considered the fine sense

and marvellous understanding [*le hault sens et merveilleux enten-
dement*] of his son Gargantua" (69; *G* 94). For reasons which are
not explained but which clearly are not imposed from without,
Gargantua decides to distance himself from excrement (or vice
versa), decides that it is something from which one should keep
oneself clean. To his father, this is an indication that Gargantua
has matured into a reasonable being: "You have more sense
[*raison*] than your years." A reasonable human being is now one
who regards excrement as European culture—nonpopular European culture—has regarded it since the end of the sixteenth
century. Gargantua, unlike the adult Pantagruel of the first novel,
has rejected a major aspect of popular culture, and his father
heartily approves.

Henceforth in *Gargantua*, excrement is no longer an "accepted part of life." Gargantua "went into some private place to
make excretion of his natural waste-products" (87; *G* 145).[8] It is
now the foolish, and certainly not the principle figures of authority, the members of the power establishment, who are put in
contact with the unclean. It is Gargantua's worthless sophist
teachers who "said that to comb or wash or clean yourself in any
other way [than with one's fingers] was to lose time in this
world" (81–82; *G* 131). It is the "Sorbonicoles" who, out of
spite when their suit against Janotus de Bragmardo is delayed in
court, "made a vow not to clean off their dirt" (80; *G* 128). The
unclean in general, and excrement in particular, is definitely
now viewed in a different light. It degrades, and is excluded
from contact with figures of authority.[9] Concurrent with this exclusion of the unclean is a new emphasis on personal hygiene.
After Gargantua finishes his gymnastics, he is "rubbed, washed,
and refreshed by a change of clothes" (91; *G* 153). After returning from battle, he is depicted "changing his clothes and passing
a comb through his hair" (119; *G* 213). There is really no equivalent for this concern with cleanliness in *Pantagruel*. In short, the
values and views of popular culture on the acceptability of dirt
in general and excrement in particular, so clearly evident in
Pantagruel, have just as clearly been excluded from *Gargantua* by
the midpoint of the novel.[10]

The same holds true of the presence of disease and infection
in the two novels. Bakhtin declared that in popular culture (and

hence in Rabelais) "gout and syphilis are 'gay diseases.' . . . They are essentially connected with the material bodily lower stratum" (B 161).[11] Though disease does not play an important part in *Pantagruel*, it is certainly true that it has no particularly negative connotations. When Nasier declares that "all sweat is salt," he adds: "Which you will admit to be true if you taste your own, or that of pox-patients when they make them sweat. It is all one to me" (176; *P* 18). Showing up for Pantagruel's fight with Loupgarou, Panurge, "imitating a man who has had the pox, twisted his gullet and contorted his fingers" (261; *P* 152). No one sends him away; rather, the others watching the fight allow him to join them.

Such equanimity is not shared in *Gargantua*. In the very liminary *dizain*, the author promises that the following book "contains no foul infection" (*ne contient mal ne infection*) (36; *G* 7).[12] It is Thubal Holoferne, Gargantua's terrible first teacher, who "died [when] in the year fourteen twenty he caught the pox" (70; *G* 97). Indeed, sophists in general are condemned as those who "corrupted all the flower of youth" (71; *G* 99). Grandgousier censures those who call for pilgrimages as a way to ward off plagues, accusing them of spreading "diabolical preachings which infect the souls of poor and simple people" (137; *G* 255). And the particular plague in question comes in for some significant association. "The priests, curates, preachers, physicians, surgeons, and apothecaries who went to visit, dress, heal, preach to, and admonish the sick had all died of the infection." But the invading Lerneans, who pillage and murder their way through Utopie, "never take any harm." "What is the reason for that, gentlemen?" the narrator asks; "Consider the problem, I beg of you" (97; *G* 167). The plague here is clearly being associated with the "bad" invaders and the disorder they bring (as opposed to the "good" curates, priests, etc.). Not surprisingly, those tainted by infection are excluded from the utopian world of Theleme that concludes the novel. The sign over the entrance reads, in part: "Enter not here . . . you with your sores, gnawed to the bone by pox, / Take your ulcers elsewhere and show them to others, / Scabby from head to toe and brimful of dishonour" (154; *G* 291). Like excrement and the unclean, disease and infection have clearly become *non gratae* with *Gargantua*, showing once again a rejection of the popular-culture values that had held sway in *Pantagruel*.[13]

Nowhere is this clearer than with the respective treatments of sex. Sex and things having to do with the genital organs are, like excrement, an important feature of Bakhtin's material bodily lower stratum and hence of his description of the imagery of popular culture. Nor would modern historians dispute that sex figured more prominently in manifestations of popular culture than in the discourse and literary production (if not in the lives) of the learned, the powerful, and the elite. One of the reasons for this is obvious. Because of their living conditions, sex was not something that the poor could have hidden, even if they had wanted to. Much like the working families in *Germinal* and other Naturalistic novels, the poor of the sixteenth century generally lived in one room, parents, children, everyone, sometimes all sharing one bed. There was no way to keep sex private, hidden; it was very much a part of everyone's everyday life.

As it is in *Pantagruel*. Recounting the swellings brought on by the eating of the great medlars, the narrator includes mention of how some individuals

grew in the length of that member which is called Nature's labourer, so that it grew marvellously long, big, stout, fat, lusty, and proud, after the ancient fashion, so much so that men made use of it as a belt, twisting it four or five times round the body. But if it happened to be in good fettle and sailing before the wind, you would have said when you saw them that such men had their lances couched for jousting at the quintain. [172; *P* 11][14]

The title character certainly demonstrates a healthy enjoyment of sex, which the narrator (and the author) shows no reticence about mentioning. Pantagruel "came to Avignon, and had not been there three days before he was in love," an expression whose precise meaning the narrator immediately clarifies: "for the women there love to play the two-backed beast" (182; *P* 29). In Paris, Pantagruel decides to pay a visit to "la Follie Gobelin" (218; *P* 81), which, according to Pierre Jourda, was a "house of pleasure."[15] When, about to return to Utopie to defend his homeland against the invading Dipsodians, Pantagruel receives a message ("Say, false lover, why have you abandoned me?") from "a Parisian lady, whom he had kept as his mistress for some time" (246; *P* 127), "this depressed him, and he would gladly have returned to Paris to make his peace with her" (247; *P* 130). Epistemon must recite the story of Dido and Aeneas in order to persuade Pantagruel to overcome his thoughts of the woman and sail back home.

Still, Pantagruel's interest (and participation) in sex pales next to that of his companion. From the very beginning, Panurge seems to talk about little else.[16] Recounting his escape from being roasted alive by a Turk, he notes that "a young English girl [?—*une jeune tudesque*], who had brought me a pot of round mirobolan plums, conserved in their manner . . . looked at my poor fly-bitten devil [*haire*], which was just as it had been taken from the fire, for it then hung down no further than my knees" (217; *P* 80). (In arranging his escape, Panurge had "thrown [a firebrand] into my rascally roaster's lap [which] burnt his whole groin [*le penil*] and began to catch his balls" [215; *P* 77].) Returning with Pantagruel from La Follie Gobelin, Panurge offers his plan for inexpensively fortifying the city of Paris: since he has found that "in this country the thing-o'-my-bobs of the women are cheaper than the stone," he suggests that "the walls ought to be built of them" (219; *P* 83). He sees only one problem with this idea, however: "The flies are marvellously fond of them [the 'thing-o'-my-bobs']. They would quickly gather round and leave their excretion there, and then all the work would be spoilt." This promptly leads him to suggest a remedy: the "thing-o'-my-bobs" "must be swatted with fine fox-tails." This remedy, in turn, sets him off on an illustrative and highly erotic tale about a fox, a lion, and an old woman (219–21; *P* 84–87). When Pantagruel questions Panurge's opening assertion concerning the morals of Parisian women, Panurge responds with yet another exemplary and erotic anecdote, this one about a man and two girls (221; *P* 87–88). Pantagruel enjoys these tales so much that, at the end of the last one, he exclaims: "Truly . . . you're a jolly companion. I should like to put you in my livery" (221; *P* 88).[17]

Indeed, Panurge is brimming with salacious tales. When explaining how he spent the money that he stole from church poor boxes, he recounts how he bribed men to marry ugly old prostitutes and then brought suit against women who wore blouses that altogether hid their breasts (228–29; *P* 98–100). When Pantagruel asks why French leagues are shorter than those in other countries, Panurge replies with an erotic story about copulating milestone distributors (245; *P* 126–27). Having heard this "historical explanation," Pantagruel "gladly accepted it." When the captured Dipsodian soldier informs Pantagruel and his men that Anarche's troops are accompanied by "a hundred and fifty thousand whores, as fair as goddesses," Panurge announces his intention to "lay out all the whores who are there this afternoon, so that not one escapes without my taking care of her." "And the good Pantagruel laughed at all this," the narrator points out (252–53; *P* 137–39). Presenting Anarche's new wife to Pantagruel, Panurge assures his master that "there is no fear of her farting . . . because she's well slit [*entommée*] . . . underneath" (272; *P* 169).

Nor is Panurge's relationship with sex all talk. Among the "thousand little devilments" that he commits with a "collection of needles and thread" is the affair of the Cordelier whose alb Panurge sewed to his cloak and shirt. As a result, when "the poor friar tried to take off his alb" at the end of the mass, "he took his gown and his shirt off with it, since they were thoroughly well sewn together, and so stripped himself to his shoulders, displaying his what-you-may-call-it [*calibistris*] to all the world"—a "calibistris," Nasier adds, that "certainly . . . was no small one" (224; *P* 93). Indeed, Nasier goes on with this anecdote at some length. (And why is it, people asked, "that friars have such long tools"? Panurge has an explanation, of course [224–25; *P* 93–94].) Like a character from a medieval morality play, Panurge wears a "codpiece . . . cut three foot long" (221; *P* 88).[18] And, of course, chapters 21–22 recount Panurge's often quite forceful attempts to "entice"—"rape" would not be an exaggeration—a married "great Parisian lady" (239–44; *P* 115–25). If the object of his affections does not succumb, it is far more the result of Panurge's cowardice than of any self-control exerted over his very sexual desires. In *Pantagruel* sex is not taboo, either for the narrator or for the characters.

As my reader might expect by now, this situation, like the others already examined, changes with and in *Gargantua*. At first, as with excrement (and, for a moment, disease), there

seems to be no difference in attitude. The narrator explains that
Gargantua came about because Grandgousier, "in the prime of
his years . . . married Gargamelle, daughter of the king of the
Butterflies, a fine, good-looking piece, and the pair of them
often played the two-backed beast, joyfully rubbing their bacon
together, to such effect that she became pregnant of a fine boy"
(46; G 31). Sometime before his fifth birthday, Gargantua "was
already beginning to exercise his codpiece"; as Nasier puts it, "it
raised its ears" (63; G 81). When he gets somewhat older, the
adolescent Gargantua "went to see the local girls [garces]" (86;
G 142) as a way of passing time after supper.

   In this respect as well, however, education makes a new man
of Grandgousier's son. When news arrives in Paris that Utopie
has been invaded, the now "educated" Gargantua immediately
sets sail for home to help (113; G 202). There is no sex-inspired
hesitation or delay, as with Pantagruel and the great Parisian
lady.[19] Indeed, from this point on, sex and Gargantua are completely separated. What little reference to sex and such matters
there is in the second half of the novel is transferred exclusively
to Friar John, who, unlike Gargantua—or, for that matter, unlike Panurge or Pantagruel in Pantagruel—is not a figure of power
and authority.[20] It is Friar John who asks why it is that "a young
woman's thighs are always cool?" (124; G 224);[21] Gargantua has
a very "learned"—and sexless—response: "That problem . . . is
neither in Aristotle, nor in Alexander of Aphrodisias, nor in
Plutarch." When Gargantua asks those assembled at a banquet
why it is "that Friar John has such a handsome nose?" the monk
responds with an explanation involving his wet-nurse's breasts
(127; G 231–32); this time it is Grandgousier who offers a sexless response: "Because . . . God wished it so, and he makes us
in such shape and to such end as pleases his divine will, even as
a potter fashions his pots." It is Friar John who tells the story
about the effect of a monk's frock on Monsieur de Meurles's
greyhound (129–30; G 239), Friar John who tells the wander-
ing pilgrims to return home and guard their spouses because the
local monks "will be having a fine fling at your wives while
you're out on your pilgrimage" (137; G 255). When Wearybones
(Lasdaller) dismisses this advice, saying that no man who saw
his wife in the daylight would bother her by night, Friar John
tells him that such a safeguard will not protect him from being

cuckolded if there are monks in the neighborhood, "for even the shadow of an abbey-steeple is fruitful" (137; *G* 256); Gargantua follows this remark with: "It's like the Nile waters in Egypt, if you believe Strabo . . . and Pliny, in the third chapter of his seventh book." Despite all these remarks, Friar John's involvement with the erotic never goes beyond words. There is never any violence involved, as between Panurge and the "great Parisian lady"; never does Friar John's conduct suggest that he is being ruled by sexual desire.[22] In the Abbey of Theleme, the description of which constitutes the closing chapters of the novel, sex may even be absent.[23]

Friar John's sexual remarks are all made at the banquet that Grandgousier holds for his son and the latter's men after Gargantua demolishes the enemy-held Gué de Vede chateau. Since banquets figure prominently in both *Pantagruel* and *Gargantua*, and since Bakhtin devotes an entire chapter to "Banquet Imagery in Rabelais," it is worth examining the "prandial passages" in these two novels carefully.

According to Bakhtin, "the banquet images . . . are closely linked in Rabelais' novel with . . . popular-festive forms" (B 278). All the elements of Bakhtinian popular culture are associated with the Rabelaisian banquet: "the limits between men and the world are erased" (B 281), "the banquet images liberate speech, lending it a fearless and free tone" (B 296), and so on. Bakhtin spends the entire chapter talking about banquets in other works of literature, mentioning *Gargantua and Pantagruel* at the beginning only to list several of the novels' banquet scenes (B 279–80). If one examines the various banquets in the first two novels, however, one can see, here as elsewhere, that a definite change takes place.

There are several passing allusions to banquets in *Pantagruel*. When the baby giant smashes his legs through the foot of his crib and, touching his feet to the ground, proceeds to walk off with the crib still around him like a tortoise in its shell, he goes in search of his father and finds him "giving a grand banquet to all the princes of his court" (180; *P* 25). While in Poitiers "pursuing his studies," Pantagruel sets up the Pierre levée, "so that [the local university] scholars could enjoy themselves by climbing on it and there banqueting with plenty of flagons, hams and pies" (181; *P* 27). After Pantagruel "resolves" the dispute between Humevesne and Baisecul, the thankful court sends the young giant a large shipment of wine. Pantagruel's companions share in the drinking of it, making for something of a banquet, and during this episode Panurge tells the occasionally off-color story of his capture and escape from the Turks. After the "sign debate" between Panurge and Thaumaste, Pantagruel takes the latter (and presumably the former and his companions) for some substantial eating and drinking (238–39; *P* 115). Later, when Pantagruel is engaged in his very serious fight with Loupgarou, Anarche and the other Dipsodian giants, who are watching from the sidelines, indulge in a banquet to which they invite Panurge and his companions (261; *P* 152).

In addition to these passing descriptions of banqueting, there are two major banquet scenes in Rabelais's first novel. Having defeated and roasted 659 of the Dipsodian cavalrymen who had approached to fight them as they first landed back in Utopie, Pantagruel and his men set up a celebratory banquet. It is, in many ways, a perfect example of Bakhtin's popular culture banquet. Limits between man and man (if not between "man and the world") are, by and large, suspended. The one survivor of the Dipsodian cavalry is invited to participate with the Utopians as an equal (250; *P* 134). When Panurge, to punctuate one of his obscene remarks, gives "a fart, a leap, and a whistle," Pantagruel, the Prince of Utopie and leader of the army, "tried to do the same" (255; *P* 143). Here indeed, "prandial speech is a free and jocular speech" (B 284); when the surviving Dipsodian soldier mentions that Anarche's army is accompanied by a large band of prostitutes, Panurge and his companions vie with each other in boasting about how they will put these women to good use (252–53; *P* 137–39).

The second major banquet takes place after Epistemon has been brought back to life by Panurge. It is during this celebration that Panurge humiliates Anarche by turning him into a hawker of green sauce (much to Pantagruel's delight) and announces that "these accursed kings are absolute dolts. They know nothing, and they're good for nothing except harming their poor subjects, and troubling the whole world with wars, for their wicked and detestable pleasure" (271; *P* 168; this is obviously an important passage, to which I will return later). In both instances, banquets certainly seem to be associated with a "democratic spirit" (B 297), or at least with the themes of Carnival previously noted.

There are also several banquet sequences in *Gargantua*, but they are separated from those in *Pantagruel* by important differences. During the final days of Gargamelle's pregnancy, Grandgousier invites people from the vicinity to a large feast, after the completion of which everyone retires to a nearby grove for dancing (and more drinking). The remarks made by the participants certainly constitute "free and jocular speech" (cf. in particular 49–50; *G* 41–43), but there is never any indication that the lord and lady of the manor are among the interlocutors or that they join in the general dancing and merriment. Similarly, when Jobelin Bridé is dismissed as Gargantua's tutor, he is given wine to drink (72; *G* 102), as is Janotus de Bragmardo at the end of his harangue (79; *G* 125); in neither case, however, is there any indication that Grandgousier or Gargantua (or anyone else) joins them in their consumption of the alcohol. Don Philippe des Marays demonstrates the advantages of the "new education" to Grandgousier in the person of Eudemon while the two lords are dining together (71; *G* 100), but there is no indication that anyone other than these two lords are sitting at the meal table—not even Eudemon, who, since he has to be summoned by des Marays, obviously is not already dining with Grandgousier and his noble guest. When, during the course of his education-filled days under Ponocrates, Gargantua occasionally takes time out for meals, there is no indication that he is joined by anyone other than his tutor (88, 91; *G* 146–48, 154). Since he spends the time going over the material already covered that day, it is certainly unlikely that he is accompanied by a group of free-talking partiers.

This is true even of Ponocrates and Gargantua's once-a-month "holiday" in the country (93; *G* 158–59). Though there is much drinking, dancing, and the like, there is no mention of any other participants, or any sort of "free tone." Again, time is spent relating even these holiday activities to passages in Greek and Latin works that figure in Gargantua's educational program.

Banqueting continues to figure in the second half of *Gargantua*, that devoted to the Picrocholine War, but again, it is very different from the festive repasts in Bakhtin's depiction of popular culture (or in *Pantagruel*). Picrochole is described as being at dinner when he orders the assault on Grandgousier's lands (96; *G* 165). On the other hand, when Grandgousier gathers his counselors together to decide how to handle this invasion and then issues his orders, there is no mention of eating (102; *G* 179).

After Gargantua has demolished the Gué de Vede chateau, which had been occupied by some of Picrochole's troops, he returns to his father's house, and Grandgousier sets up a large celebratory banquet. Friar John there makes the various off-color remarks cited above, but no one else follows his lead. Indeed, as already mentioned, Grandgousier and Gargantua sometimes respond to his comments with highly learned, completely "nonpopular" remarks of their own. After the war has been brought to a conclusion, Grandgousier sets up a second victory feast for Gargantua and his companions (149; *G* 279). This time, not even Friar John introduces "free and jocular speech."

Though Bakhtin never actually examines the banquet passages in Rabelais's texts in his chapter entitled "Banquet Imagery in Rabelais," it is clear that, on this point as well, there is a major change from the first to the second novel. While it is true that banquets in *Pantagruel*—and in particular the one held after the defeat of the 659 Dipsodian cavalrymen—do seem to be characterized by a spirit of equality and freedom akin to that in popular culture banquet imagery, this spirit appears to be almost entirely absent from the group dinners in *Gargantua*. When, at one festive repast in the second book, a character actually employs the "free and jocular" language that Bakhtin (rightly, I believe) describes as being typical of popular culture "prandial speech," no one follows his lead. Grandgousier does not seem to participate with his tipsy guests in their exchange of uninhibited pleasantries before Gargantua's birth. He does not join Jobelin Bridé in the latter's drinking, just as his son does not join Janotus de Bragmardo in his. This is a great change from the banquet in *Pantagruel*, during which everyone joined in the talk about how to treat the Dipsodian prostitutes and Prince Pantagruel did not hesitate to imitate Panurge when the latter "gave a fart, a leap, and a whistle."[24] The atmosphere of egalitarian freedom which evidently typified the popular culture banquet has almost entirely disappeared, along with so much else, in the move from *Pantagruel* to *Gargantua*.

As I have tried to demonstrate, popular culture—its way of

viewing the world, its basic imagery—is methodically and systematically excluded from *Gargantua*, either before the work
ever gets underway or during the course of the narrative's development. This exclusion culminates in the utopian, but completely "unpopular," Abbey of Theleme. Though he generally
managed to contort even the most unlikely passages in *Gargantua and Pantagruel* into proof texts for his interpretation, Bakhtin
to an extent acknowledged this development himself when he
wrote that Theleme "is fundamentally linked with the aristocratic movements of the Renaissance. This is not a popular-
festive mood but a court and humanist utopia, which has rather
the flavor of Princess Marguerite's circles than that of the
marketplace" (B 138–39). Since Bakhtin had already decided
what the "essence" of Rabelais was, his reaction to Theleme was
inevitable: "Theleme is characteristic neither of Rabelais' philosophy nor of his system of images, nor of his style. . . . Theleme is
not in line with Rabelais' imagery and style" (B 138, 139).

As I have attempted to demonstrate with my comparisons of
Pantagruel and *Gargantua*, on the points of "general" popular
culture, excrement, disease, sex, and the banquet, Bakhtin is
quite simply wrong. Theleme is certainly not in line with *Pantagruel*; in fact, one can assert with almost virtual certainty that
the protagonists in Rabelais's first novel, Pantagruel and Panurge,
would not have been allowed in. On the other hand, Theleme
seems a very logical conclusion to the systematic exclusion of
popular culture that goes on before and during *Gargantua*.
Theleme may not be characteristic of *Pantagruel*, but it is certainly in line with the development of the second novel after the
episodes of the arse-wipe and Gargantua's education under
Ponocrates. Bakhtin's "Rabelais" is unchanging, every bit as
fixed and monolithic—if, admittedly, not as serious—as the
"official culture" that Bakhtin condemns (but then, medieval
and Renaissance "official culture" was not as serious as Bakhtin
maintained, either). But the real "Rabelais"—the text of *Gargantua and Pantagruel*—does change, radically. The more it
changes, the wider the gap becomes between it and Bakhtin's
interpretation.

This change from *Pantagruel* to *Gargantua* is particularly well-
illustrated by the absence in the latter of an equivalent for the

episode that seemingly should have been carried over from the former but was not: Epistemon's description of the underworld.

Many critics have noted the often quite striking repetitions of material from *Pantagruel* to *Gargantua*. Like the first, the second novel recounts the (fantastic) birth, childhood, adolescent education, and first military adventures of a giant. In each narrative, the hostilities of the second half are initiated by some other people who move beyond their own frontiers and invade those of the protagonist: in *Pantagruel*, "the Dipsodes had crossed their frontiers, devastated a great tract of Utopie" (245; *P* 126); in *Gargantua*, "all Picrochole's advisers, officers, and servants . . . incited, encouraged, or counselled him to cross his frontier for the purpose of troubling [the Utopians]" (148; *G* 277). In *Gargantua*, as in *Pantagruel*, the protagonist returns home from Paris, where he had been studying, to lead his father's troops and protect his country against these invaders. In each narrative, the protagonist learns information about the invaders from an enemy soldier: in *Pantagruel*, from the one survivor of the 660 Dipsodian cavalrymen burned by Panurge; in *Gargantua*, from Touchspigot (Toucquedillon), whom Friar John took prisoner. In *Pantagruel*, Pantagruel mows down enemy soldiers with the corpse of the giant Loupgarou, while Panurge, Carpalim, and Eusthenes "cut the throats of [*esgorgetoient*] all those that were knocked to the ground" (264; *P* 157); in *Gargantua*, Friar John mows down the Lerneans who invade the Abbey of Seuillé with a giant cross, while his fellow monks "slit the throats of [*esguorgetassent*] those lying on the ground" (100; *G* 174). In *Pantagruel*, Alcofribas Nasier at the end of the war wanders by mistake into the world inside Pantagruel's mouth; in *Gargantua*, six or five pilgrims hiding from the war are consumed by Gargantua as part of a salad and wander around inside his mouth for some time before they can make their escape. In each narrative the war comes to a conclusion after the protagonist defeats the invaders in one great battle. It is not surprising, given all these repetitions, that one critic went so far as to ask: "Is *Gargantua* a reworking of *Pantagruel*?"[25]

Why did Rabelais repeat so many elements of *Pantagruel* in *Gargantua*, and in so obvious a fashion? We have no personal correspondence that touches on this matter, no theoretical works, nothing that a critic can use to *prove* his explanations. One thing we would seem to be able to say for sure, however, is that if Rabelais repeated elements of *Pantagruel* in *Gargantua*, it was not because he lacked the imagination to devise new scenes. Since he fills *Gargantua* with very clear reminiscences of *Pantagruel*, which had just appeared a few years before, since, in fact, he begins *Gargantua* (41; *G* 19) by telling his readers to look back at *Pantagruel*, it seems possible that he might have included the very specific echoes of *Pantagruel* in *Gargantua* at least in part to cause the reader to recall the first text while reading the second.

If one compares *Gargantua* with *Pantagruel*, one is bound to be struck in a rather complicated way by a strange feature of Rabelais's second text. In *Pantagruel*, the hero's tutor, Epistemon, is killed during the war with the Lerneans, only to be brought back to life by Panurge. "Now [Epistemon] began to speak, saying that he had seen the devils, and held intimate conversation with Lucifer, and feasted both in hell and in the Elysian Fields." The pedagogue goes on to give a detailed description of everything and everyone he saw during his brief sojourn in the underworld (265−70; *P* 158−65). In *Gargantua*, the hero's tutor, Ponocrates, is also killed in combat: "Gargantua first called a roll of his men, and discovered that there had been few casualties in the battle—in fact only some foot-soldiers of Captain Tolmere's company, and Ponocrates, who had received an arquebus shot in his doublet" (145; *G* 271). Like Epistemon, Ponocrates is alive again several pages later: Gargantua appoints him to serve as intendant of Lerné until Picrochole's son is old enough to rule (147; *G* 276), and Grandgousier gives him the chateau of La Roche Clermaud and adjacent lands in recognition of his services during the Picrocholine War (149; *G* 279). The similarities of the two texts on this point are striking, but there is one very important difference. In *Pantagruel*, the text describes how Epistemon came back to life (Panurge sewed his head back on); in *Gargantua*, there is no explanation whatsoever. On page 145 Ponocrates is dead; on pages 147 and 149 he is quite alive.

Why? The answer that first springs to mind is the obvious one: Rabelais made a mistake, an oversight. In a rush to complete his narrative, he continued to treat Ponocrates as alive because he forgot that he had killed him off.[26] This explanation is not as patent as it might first appear, however. *Gargantua* went through at least ten editions between 1535 and 1542, several of which Rabelais himself supervised and revised with great care.[27] In each of these editions, Ponocrates is listed among the war casualties, only to reappear, alive, just a few pages later. It is possible to assert that Rabelais at first made an oversight, but it is virtually impossible to argue that it was by oversight that this inconsistency remained in the text. If Ponocrates is listed as dead on 145 and then alive on 147 and 149, Rabelais must have wanted it this way. Why?

To an extent, such an apparent contradiction must be understood as yet another manifestation of the narrator's persona, a character who delights in nothing so much as making fun of the reader. From the very beginning of Rabelais's second novel, the narrator constantly affirms one thing with the greatest of vigor and apparent sincerity, only to announce moments later that he puts no credence whatsoever in his previous affirmation and that anyone who does must indeed be a simpleton. As Gérard Defaux has demonstrated, Alcofribas Nasier in this respect allows Rabelais to continue the depiction and critique of misused learning ("sophistry") that he had first developed to a great extent with Panurge in *Pantagruel*.[28]

Indeed, it could be argued that the resurrection of Ponocrates is a particularly good example of the likening of the *Gargantua* Alcofribas Nasier to the *Pantagruel* Panurge. Since no character in the second narrative is shown resuscitating Ponocrates, one could maintain that it is the narrator himself, Nasier, who brings about the revival of the pedagogue, a revival achieved in the first narrative by Panurge.

One might also view Ponocrates' unexplained resurrection from the perspective offered by a lesser Rabelais scholar. In the first half of the novel, the narrator repeatedly presents himself as a "modern" historiographer, someone who writes, not like the old chroniclers, simply repeating oft-told legends, but rather as a serious, scientific research scholar, someone who hunts for and checks his facts in archives, personal interviews with witnesses, and so forth. Yet this "model of a modern historiographer," for all that he has followed the procedures of "scientific historiography" advocated by Jean Bodin and other sixteenth-century theorists of the "new," "perfect" historiography, makes mistakes and blunders in his reconstruction of Gargantua's biography, suggesting that even the most scientific, objective methodology for the presentation of the past cannot overcome the problems posed by the subjective, human limitations of the historian who must put that methodology into practice.[29] In this light, Ponocrates' "death" and subsequent "rebirth" may have been meant as yet another example in Rabelais's argument that modern historians, for all their vaunted objective, scientific methodology, must still be viewed by readers of historiography as human, and hence fallible.

Still, it is very tempting to suggest that Rabelais set up the parallel with chapter 30 of *Pantagruel* in the later chapters of *Gargantua* in part, at least, in order to make readers of the second novel think back to the famous passage in the first. By this point in *Gargantua* (chaps. 49–51), the reader has encountered so many reminiscences of the first narrative that such recall would be almost automatic. In recollecting the episode of Epistemon's resurrection, however, the reader of *Gargantua* would have been struck by the absence of an equivalent of Epistemon's description of Hell. It is worth examining the pedagogue's Hell narrative in light of the preceding analysis of the changes from *Pantagruel* to *Gargantua* to see if Epistemon's description contains elements that would have made it unacceptable in Rabelais's second novel.

And indeed it does: two major elements. The first has to do with leisure time. During his brief sojourn in Hades, Epistemon sees Epictetus, who spends his time in Hell dancing under a trellis on which he has posted his motto:

> To drink and dance, to sport and play
> And drink wine, red and white,
> With nothing more to do each day
> And crowns to count each night.
> [269; *P* 164n][30]

This very positive, indeed admiring, view of the *dolce far niente* approach to life runs throughout *Pantagruel*, from the very first pages. In the Prologue, Nasier tells his readers: "So far as I am concerned, I would have every man put aside his own business [*besoingne*], take no care for his trade [*mestier*],[31] and forget his own affairs, in order to devote himself entirely to this book"— that is, the *Grandes et inestimables cronicques*, first published earlier in 1532, and to which *Pantagruel* is something of a sequel. "I would," Nasier continues, "have him allow no distraction or hindrance from elsewhere to trouble his mind" (167; *P* 4). He has written *Pantagruel*, he tells his readers, because he wanted "still further to increase your entertainment" (168; *P* 6). Both he, as he writes, and his readers, as they read him, are described as being "at leisure" (*de sejour*) (171; *P* 9).[32]

Like his chronicler, Pantagruel is a great believer in leisure time. He sets up the Pierre levée (Raised Stone) in Poitiers "so that these scholars, when they did not know what else to do, could enjoy themselves [*passassent le temps*] by climbing on it and then banqueting with plenty of flagons, hams, and pies" (181; *P* 27). In Toulouse "he learned to dance very well and to play with the two-handed sword, as is the custom of the students of that university" (182; *P* 29). In Orléans he "learnt to play tennis with [the local students], so well that he became a champion" (183; *P* 30). There he also writes the school song:

> A tennis ball in the cod-placket,
> In the hand a tennis-racket,
> Skill at the slow dance to trip it,
> And there's the Licentiate hooded.
> [183; *P* 31]

A student in name, the young Pantagruel seems to devote much more time to extracurriculars than to his books. It is not surprising that Nasier is able to earn a living in the world inside his mouth by sleeping: "for there they hire men by the day as sleepers, and you can earn five or six halfpence a time. But those who snore very loud are paid a good seven and a half" (274; *P* 173).

This preoccupation with leisure time, and this view of an ideal world as a land where one did not have to work all day in order to stay alive, was very much a feature of medieval and Renaissance popular culture. Nor was this the preoccupation and dream solely of peasants. With few exceptions, all men of the time had to work most of their lives to have a place to live, food, and clothes. This view of life as a time of work is the first thing that Nasier encounters when he enters the world inside Pantagruel's mouth. Seeing a man planting cabbages, he walks up to him and asks:

"What are you doing here, my friend?"
"I'm planting cabbages," he said.
"But how and what for?" I asked.
"Ah, sir," said he, "we can't all be rich. I earn my living this way."
[273; P 171]

The dream of a land where this is not so, where food is free and plentiful and men do not have to work to stay alive, figured in the imagery of medieval and Renaissance popular culture most often as the mythical Land of Cockaigne. Burke cites a Renaissance folk poem about this land which shows just how close to it the preoccupation with leisure in *Pantagruel* really is:

> For sleeping one hour
> Of profound sleep
> Without awakening,
> One earns six francs,
> And as much for eating,
> And for drinking well
> One earns a pistole;
> This country is funny,
> One earns ten francs a day
> For making love. [190][33]

Again, all this changes with (or in) *Gargantua*. Everything still seems the same in the opening chapter, when Nasier says: "And to give you some information about myself, who address you, I believe that I am descended from some wealthy king or prince of the olden days. For you have never met a man with a greater desire to be a king or to be rich than I have, so that I may eat well, and do no work" (41; G 21).[34] But Gargantua's education under Ponocrates makes a change quite evident. As the very chapter title tells us, "Gargantua was so disciplined by Ponocrates that he did not waste an Hour of the Day" (86; G 143; cf. 87; G 144).[35] In his exercises, Gargantua does not bother learning how to jump "at three steps and a leap . . . with a hop or with the German action [*au sault Alemant*]—for, as Gymnaste said, such leaps are useless and serve no purpose [*sont inutiles et de nul bien*] in war" (90; G 151). Most of dinner is spent repeating previous lessons, "the rest of the time being spent in good, learned, and profitable conversation [*bons propous, tous letrez et utiles*]" (91; G 154). Even Gargantua's once-a-month countryside holiday is arranged so that "although the day was spent without books or reading, it was not profitless" (93; G 159); as he wanders through the fields the young giant recites Latin bucolic poetry and translates it into French.[36]

While Gargantua is learning to make every minute count, those who do not use their time constructively are condemned. Gargantua finds no justification for the existence of "a monk—I mean those lazy monks—[who] doesn't till the fields like a peasant, nor guard the country like a soldier, nor cure the sick like a physician, nor preach and instruct the world like a good gospeller and preceptor, nor carry commodities and things that the public need like a merchant. This is the reason why everyone hoots at them and abhors them" (126; G 228–29). The change of attitude toward leisure from *Pantagruel* should be sufficiently clear. Not working is no longer admirable, a goal, and even a dream. Not working is wasting time, or at the least being "lazy."[37]

While such a change very definitely marks a movement away from the values of popular culture to those of the power establishment, it is worth clarifying the historical context of Rabelais's (or his text's) change. This condemnation of wasting time should not be seen as some sort of literary manifestation of the now infamous Protestant work ethic. To begin with, the "Protestant" work ethic—unlike the Reformed Church—did not come into being during the sixteenth century. As recent historians like André Biéler have shown, what we (through Weber, Tawney, and others) refer to as the "Protestant work ethic" was not created by Calvin and the Geneva Reformed Church. Rather, it was a development of certain Protestant cultures during the seventeenth century.[38]

Far more contemporary with Rabelais was a condemnation of leisure or vagrancy that sprang from the elite's growing concern about the greatly increased numbers of unemployed (especially urban unemployed) at the opening of the sixteenth century. The

elite found itself faced with a very real possibility that such con-
centrations of the unemployed could lead to civil disorder and
even revolt. As Muchambled remarks, "More and more the idle
stranger was regarded with fear" (156). City councils began
to pass ordinances forbidding the congregation of unemployed
within their walls (157), and by the period 1520–40 those not
working were viewed as so dangerous that they were expelled
(214). If the elite of the sixteenth century feared the idle and
condemned unemployment, it was not the result of some religious ethic, but rather, a suspicion—and, after the Peasants' War
of 1524–25, a knowledge—of what idleness among the masses
could lead to. The change of view from *Pantagruel* to *Gargantua*
on the question of leisure time certainly indicates yet another
shift from the values of popular culture to those of the contemporary power establishment.

The other major element of Epistemon's Hell narrative that
certainly would not have fit into the "nonpopular" *Gargantua* is
a very pronounced bias against power, wealth, and socioeconomic inequality. For over five pages Epistemon describes a
world in which the politically powerful and wealthy are deprived of their power and humiliated: "Alexander the Great
[was] darning old breeches for a miserable livelihood. Xerxes
was hawking mustard. Darius [was] a cleaner of cesspools, . . ."
(266–70; *P* 160–65). As Bakhtin was quick—and quite correct—to point out, this entire sequence is a classic example of
the "inverted world" image that figured so prominently in popular culture (especially at Carnival). In this image the normal
order of a world of inequalities is inverted, top to bottom and
bottom to top.

Epistemon makes the social dimension of this inversion in his
Hell quite clear himself: "Thus did those who had been great
lords in this world here gain their poor, miserable, scurvy livelihood down there," he says. "On the other hand, the philosophers and those who had been penurious [*indigens*] in this
world, had their turn at being great lords down below" (268;
P 163). There is a very clearly dyadic view of human society
here—great lords versus the penurious—under (and not very far
under) which seems to lie a very definite resentment of the great
lords' wealth and the unjustified political and economic inequality that creates and maintains it.[39]

The have-nots have never been pleased by the fact that there are haves who possess not only money and the comforts that it brings but also political power that gives them control over the have-nots and the ability to maintain their own "have" position and the very structure of socioeconomic inequality. This resentment was particularly pronounced and widespread at the opening of the sixteenth century. During the period 1340–1450, the Black Death and the Hundred Years War had devastated the peasantry. With the relative peace that followed in the second half of the fifteenth century, agriculture was able to reestablish itself, and because of the considerably reduced peasant population, it was more than able to meet the peasants' nutritional needs, and at reasonable prices. In part as a result of this cheap and abundant food, the peasantry of the second half of the fifteenth century enjoyed a relative material comfort, and the peasant population began to increase with relative rapidity. Eventually, however, the rate of growth of the peasant population overtook that of agriculture, until, by 1520, agricultural production was no longer able to keep up with the ever-increasing nutritional needs of the peasantry (Knecht 307). Concomitantly, the price of food rose, such that the purchase power of the peasantry fell by 50 percent from 1450 to 1550 (ibid. 309).

In addition, as Yves-Marie Bercé has shown, large numbers of rural inhabitants around 1500 and thereafter found themselves being crowded off the land by nobles who were acquiring more and more of the limited supply of arable countryside. Even those peasants not altogether dispossessed often no longer were able to control enough property to support themselves. By 1547 most peasants did not have enough land to serve the needs of their families (Knecht 308).

Those dispossessed of their property, and those unable to support themselves and their families from the property they were able to retain, were forced into the cities to look for work, but found only minimal—if any—employment (Bercé 223). This rapid influx of unemployed peasants into the urban centers adversely affected the economic situation of the urban lower class. According to Knecht, in fact, the reign of Francis I saw the beginning of a serious decline in the living standards of the urban proletariat (314).

All of these changes played a major role in the discontent

with growing economic inequality that has been noted among "the people" of the era (Moeller 55). Such discontent led to increasing strife between rich and poor (Bercé 223), an aggressiveness on the part of the poor that found its primary outlet and escape valve in Carnival, with its freedom of word and deed for all against all, its degradation of even the mighty by those over whom the mighty normally reigned. As Robert Muchambled, among others, has argued, Carnival provided an organized and fixed structure in which this aggression could be discharged without rupturing the cohesion of the community itself (65). Even the "haves" recognized this function of Carnival, according to Muchambled; they tolerated the disorder of Carnival because they saw it as a way of preventing greater social disruption (183).

According to some modern scholars, Carnival brought about the discharge of the people's aggression by creating a momentary egalitarian utopia; for the duration of Carnival, the have-nots forgot their feelings of resentment because they were able to move as equals with the powerful in a world where everyone was equal.[40] Whether or not this was true of the sixteenth-century carnival, it is not the nature of the inverted world of Epistemon's Hell. Rather than being a place where the downtrodden move as equals with their everyday downtreaders, Epistemon's Hell is a land of have-not revenge, where the downtreaders are now downtrodden and the once-powerless are now in a position to do some downtreading of their own.

This inverted world, so much a part of popular Carnival culture, in which the powerful are not simply rendered powerless but humiliated, is clearly and extensively expressed in Epistemon's narrative. But it also crops up elsewhere in *Pantagruel*. Anarche, the king of Dipsodie, is not simply dethroned; he is humiliated, and by a commoner. Panurge makes him a "hawker of green sauce," forcing him through a humiliating scene before Pantagruel, and then marries him to "an old whore" (271–72; *P* 167–68). (Witnessing this, Pantagruel, himself a prince, "enjoyed everything.") The woman whom Panurge humiliates before all Paris in revenge for refusing his advances is "one of the great ladies of the city" (239; *P* 116).[41] (Again, viewing her humiliation, Prince Pantagruel "found [it] very fine and original" [244; *P* 124]). Baisecul and Humevesne, both repeatedly described as "lords" (*seigneurs*), are each given a foolish speech.

At one point Panurge even makes a remark that sums up the bias against the rich and powerful which seems to underlie all these scenes (and which has been an essential part of popular culture since time immemorial): "These accursed kings are absolute dolts. They know nothing, and they're good for nothing except harming their poor subjects, and troubling the whole world with wars, for their wicked and detestable pleasure" (271; *P* 168). (Again, this is part of the passage followed by the remark, "Pantagruel enjoyed everything" [272; *P* 168].[42] Amazingly, Bakhtin never quotes this passage.)

Given this repeated emphasis on—and resentment of—socioeconomic inequality, it is not surprising that *Pantagruel* in general exhibits a strong awareness of social hierarchy. In the very first sentence of the text, the narrator introduces himself to the "most illustrious and most valorous [*treschevaleureux*] champions, noblemen, and others, who gladly devote yourselves to all gentle and honest pursuits." These people, who pass their time with "ladies and maidens" ("les honnorables dames et damoiselles"), Nasier addresses as "Lords" ("Messieurs"), while he describes himself as "your humble slave" (167–68; *P* 3–6).[43] Elsewhere Nasier speaks of "high and mighty noblemen" who have read the *Grandes et inestimables cronicques* (167; *P* 4). Not surprisingly, he refers to Pantagruel as "my master" (174; *P* 15), "my lord and master" (277; *P* 177), and "the noble Pantagruel" (181; *P* 27). *Pantagruel* expresses anything but a "carnivalesque" suspension of hierarchical rank (B 10).

In *Gargantua*, it is otherwise. Emphasis on social structure and hierarchy has almost completely disappeared: the work is no longer addressed to "gentlemen" (i.e., nobles), but rather to classless "boozers" and "poxy friends" (*verolés*) (37; *G* 9). Readers are no longer addressed as "Messieurs"; Nasier no longer refers to himself as "your humble slave." When nobles or aristocrats do figure in the text, they are treated with a respect certainly lacking in *Pantagruel*. Arpharbal, the defeated King of Canarre, is treated "courteously and kindly . . . with incredible generosity [*avec incroyable debonnaireté*]" (146; *G* 273) by Grandgousier.[44] The only possibly slighting reference to nobility, the bracketed part of the narrator's comment, "foreigners marvel at the patience [or, to be more precise, the stupidity] of France's kings" (75; *G* 111), was promptly excised with the second 1535 edition. There are no complaints in *Gargantua* about how kings make life miserable for the people, no remarks about the miserable lot of the poor, no division of men into "noble lords" and "the penurious" with a discontented perspective emanating from the latter. In short, the narrative (and, hence, the author) of *Gargantua* by and large leaves the dominant class alone; when it does bring them in, it treats them—or shows them treated—with respect.[45] It is obvious that on yet another front the point of view of Rabelais's text has shifted; unlike *Pantagruel*, *Gargantua* does not give voice to the (at times resentful) feelings of popular culture. The second novel does not necessarily go so far as to espouse the perspective and values of the power establishment, but it is certainly respectful of these values and the class whose members hold them.

As the preceding several pages should have made clear, Epistemon's Hell narrative, though very characteristic of *Pantagruel*, would not have fit into *Gargantua*. Its views on leisure and laziness and its disapproving awareness of socioeconomic inequality, expressed throughout the first novel and very much a part of popular culture, could have had no place in the second narrative, from which these views and this disapproving awareness, along with the culture of which they were a part, are so systematically excluded. In the case of Epistemon's narrative the exclusion seems to be anything but surreptitious, however. Given the number of parallels with or echoes of the setting of that narrative in *Gargantua*, one is very tempted to suggest that Rabelais very purposely went out of his way to cause his readers to notice the changes he was making with his second novel, the aspects of the first that he was forsaking.[46] Though I have no reason to believe that Rabelais ever sketched a Hell narrative for Ponocrates, I do believe that he wanted his readers to notice that—and consider why—such a passage was absent from its so carefully arranged setting in *Gargantua*.

The preceding pages should have made it clear to even the most fervent Bakhtinian that there is a major change from *Pantagruel* to *Gargantua* on the acceptance of popular culture, its values and its views. Bakhtin's interpretation of Rabelais provides an unbalanced (and often contorted) presentation of the first novel, but still one that has some basis in Rabelais's text and does shed some light on the work in question; "Bakhtin's Rabelais" has almost nothing to do with the second narrative, however, and can only blind readers to what is actually going on in the book that François Rabelais published in 1535.

The preceding pages should have done something else as well. After all these examples on all these various points, the reader should certainly be asking why Rabelais in 1535 so methodically rejected and excluded a culture, a set of values, and a world view that he had accepted so fully into his narrative discourse only two or three years before.

There are no definite answers, of course. We have virtually no extratextual evidence to verify explanations of such changes, explanations that of necessity involve determining the motivations of a specific historical personage into whose thoughts we have almost no access other than *Gargantua and Pantagruel* itself. This is no reason to abandon proposing interpretations, however. There is, indeed, enough secondary material to allow for several "valid" (as E. D. Hirsch uses the term) explanations.

2

The Historical Context of
Rabelais's Changing Attitude
toward Popular Culture

The change from *Pantagruel* to *Gargantua* can be seen against, and as a reflection of, the changing relationship to popular culture of the learned, the powerful, and the elite that was a very real phenomenon of the sixteenth century, a historical development that has been the subject of considerable study and documentation by scholars writing during the last few decades. As Burke, Muchambled, and others have shown, this change operated on two fronts.

On the one hand, the establishment churches, and especially the Roman Catholic church, attacked popular culture both because they saw it (quite correctly) to be a repository of pagan beliefs and because they regarded it to be an indulgence in licentiousness (Muchambled 209). The first of these reasons must have had something to do with the Renaissance rediscovery and awareness of antiquity; the more scholars learned about the cultures of past civilizations, the more sixteenth-century men— including clerics—would have seen the similarities between popular culture and pagan civilization. The second reason must have owed more to the Renaissance's chronological sibling, the Reformation. One of the main issues on which Luther, Calvin, and other Reformers attacked the Catholic church was the immorality of its prelates. As a result, much of the Counter-Reformation (as well, of course, as the Reformation) involved the condemnation and expulsion of hitherto tolerated moral license. Both of these objections to popular culture appear in the Roman Catholic church's treatment of festivals. As Robert Muchambled has shown, the Catholic church went so far as to convert popular festivals into religious processions (158), striking from them in the process the paganism and licentiousness which sixteenth-century Reformers had condemned as having no part in the Christian sacred.[1]

The other front on which the rejection of popular culture operated during the sixteenth century was the aristocratic, that of the secular upper class. The writings of Castiglione and other Italian humanists had a real influence on the economic and political elite, who did indeed reject the universal participation in popular culture of their ancestors in order to adhere to and develop a separate, "refined" culture of their own (Burke 271). Burke offers one possible explanation for this change: "As their military role declined, the nobility had to find other ways of justifying their privileges: they had to show they were different from other people. The polished manners of the nobility were imitated by officials, lawyers and merchants who wanted to pass for noblemen.[2] The withdrawal of all these groups from popular culture was more complete because it included their wives and daughters, who had long performed the function of mediators" (271–72).

Different historians stress different factors to explain why this two-fronted rejection of popular culture was carried out so thoroughly during the sixteenth century but not before. Muchambled emphasizes that before 1500 neither the state nor the church had sufficient power, was sufficiently centralized, to impress its will to any great extent on the populace (22). Burke acknowledges that some sporadic attempts at rejection, or at least modification, of popular culture were made by church and state during the Middle Ages (218), but stresses that these reforms were not undertaken in a systematic and thus effective fashion until the sixteenth century because the views and values that lay behind them were largely the result of Renaissance and Reformation (271). To these general impetuses can be added two very specifically datable ones: the Peasants' War of 1524/25 and the Anabaptist takeover of Münster in 1534/35.[3] These events, both of which received great attention throughout Europe, demonstrated graphically to those in power the hostile and even dangerous side of the people. As Carlo Ginzburg has written, the

Peasants' War and the reign of the Anabaptists in Münster con-
stituted a "decisive crisis" in the "increasingly rigid distinction
between the culture of the dominant classes and artisan and
peasant cultures." "At that time, while maintaining and even
emphasizing the distance between the classes, the necessity of
reconquering, ideologically as well as physically, the masses
threatening to break loose from every sort of control from above
was dramatically brought home to the dominant classes" (126).
If the power establishment began to reject and condemn popular
culture in the sixteenth century, it was out of fear as much as out
of disdain or disapproval.[4]

The change from *Pantagruel* to *Gargantua* is therefore very
much consistent with contemporary developments in the culture of the dominant classes. Still, these developments did not
occur instantaneously, but rather, over a period of several decades, while the very marked and almost complete change from
Pantagruel to the second half of *Gargantua* is contained within
two or, at the most, three years. Certain devotees of the old
Geistesgeschichte approach to literature—or aficionados of the
newer post–Foucault *epistemè* "methodology"—might be satisfied with the preceding several pages of explanation, but it is difficult, at least for me, to accept them as a sufficient accounting
for the sudden change between *Pantagruel* and *Gargantua*. If this
development in the thinking of the upper classes was already
underway before 1532 (the date of *Pantagruel*), as it most certainly was,[5] why did Rabelais include so much popular culture
in his first novel? Why did he then demonstrate so thorough an
awareness of and concern with this development, of which he
had just shown such a complete unawareness or lack of concern,
only a few years later in his second narrative? Biographical criticism, unless presented under the guise of psychoanalysis, is very
much out of fashion these days, but I believe that answers to this
question may be found by paying some attention to events in the
life of the author contemporary with the publication of his first
two narratives.

We know very little about the life of François Rabelais. There
does not yet exist—and probably never will—a solid, detailed
biography, something similar to Donald Frame's life of Montaigne, because we simply do not have enough information

about Rabelais.[6] Fortunately for the purposes of this discussion, the years 1532–35 are among the best documented of Rabelais's poorly documented life. We know that by mid-1532, Rabelais was practicing medicine in Lyons, augmenting his income (and/or his reputation) by publishing scholarly editions of Greek and Latin medical texts. In the summer or fall, the first edition of *Pantagruel* was published, and by 1 November its author was appointed physician at the Hôtel-Dieu.

Between his scholarly publications and his practice, Rabelais evidently made a good name for himself as a physician, for when Bishop Jean du Bellay, an important figure in the ecclesiastical-political hierarchy of the time, set off for Rome in January of 1534 to serve as Francis I's ambassador to the Papal Curia, he took Rabelais along with him as his personal physician.[7] Rabelais arrived in Rome on 2 February and left during the following month, being back in Lyons by 14 April. During the years to come he several times returned to Italy, but these sojourns came after the first publication of *Gargantua*, and so do not concern us here. Rather, here it is a question of what Rabelais would have encountered during his first journey, both in Italy and in Bishop du Bellay's entourage, that might have influenced him to alter his "style" from *Pantagruel* to *Gargantua*. Since du Bellay's entourage is a more limited and specific subject than Renaissance Italy, it is perhaps better dealt with first.

Before Rabelais ever arrived in Rome, he encountered a world different from that—or those—that he had already known: the court of a great French nobleman. Prior to January 1534, Rabelais's only sustained association with nobility had been his term as personal secretary to Geoffroy d'Estissac, bishop of Maillezais (1524–26). D'Estissac, though a noble, had little to do with the French royal court and the recent developments in "noble thought." According to Heulhard, the bishop of Maillezais did not enjoy life at court, spent as little time there as possible, and usually resided on his properties in Poitou.[8] Rabelais's other distinguished acquaintances from the period before 1534, such as the jurist André Tiraqueau, were important in their own world, but they were not closely associated with the royal court or the principal centers of humanistic endeavor.

Jean du Bellay, on the other hand, certainly was. A central figure at the court of Francis I, a member of one of France's most distinguished noble families, and a powerful figure in the Catholic church, he would have been aware of the most recent developments in aristocratic, upper-class thought. There is every reason to believe that he would have continued French royal court life and its culture in his own considerable entourage. His correspondence is that of a very sober-minded individual. There are no crude jokes, no salacious gossip about members of the papal court (though there was ample material for such should he have cared to report it). Therefore, when Rabelais entered du Bellay's entourage as a physician, he came in contact with—and no doubt had to conform to—the life-style and views of the new "refined" European upper class for the first time. Much of what had been allowed, and even applauded, in previous French royal courts, such as that which accompanied Charles VIII to Italy at the end of the preceding century, was no longer to be found in this modern court society.[9] For most of the rest of his life, Rabelais lived within the sphere of such court life, as physician either to Bishop (later Cardinal) Jean du Bellay or to his brother, Guillaume du Bellay, seigneur de Langey, one of Francis I's great military leaders, later military governor of the Piedmont.

If *Gargantua*, of 1535, shows a sudden awareness of and response to the social and behavioral trends of the European elite, it must, in part, be the result of Rabelais's sudden entrance into a world previously unknown to him. Whether or not he was concerned specifically about how the bishop himself might react to his narrative, Rabelais would have developed in the bishop's circle a new understanding of what it meant to be a member of the upper class, to write as a member of that class for other members of the same class.

I do not believe it to be a function of literary criticism to defend works of literature against moral judgments, just as I do not believe it to be a function of the critic to construe such judgments. Nevertheless, given the very strong reactions that the preceding explanation of the shift from *Pantagruel* to *Gargantua* has provoked in some listeners to previous presentations of my argument, who have been moved to condemn Rabelais with terms such as "wimp" and "toady," I feel that I should take a moment here to make the clearest possible explanation—defense, if you will—of Rabelais's action.

First, it should be repeatedly and heavily emphasized that Rabelais would have seen himself as—was, in fact—very much a part of the upper class himself, long before he joined Bishop du Bellay for that first journey to Rome. It is true that with his entrance into du Bellay's entourage, Rabelais for the first time moved in the world of the politically and socially great and powerful. But while he no doubt saw this entrance as an improvement in his life, Rabelais would not have seen it in any way as a transition on his part from a popular to an establishment milieu. A trained and already distinguished physician, someone who studied law and moved in the circle of at least one eminent jurist (Tiraqueau), a student of the classics who had corresponded in Latin and Greek with Budé and Erasmus, Rabelais must have seen himself as an eminently qualified participant in learned culture long before 1534. If he included popular culture in *Pantagruel* in 1532, it was as a member of the elite and as part of their long-standing bi-culturalism; even in this first novel Rabelais did not embrace popular culture to the exclusion of its learned counterpart. If he abandoned the former in *Gargantua*, Rabelais was not changing ("betraying") his original cultural allegiance, but rather reaffirming it with an awareness and expression of how that culture was changing and redefining itself.

Neither can one fairly accuse Rabelais of co-opting popular culture, of including it in learned discourse only to defuse it, to sanitize it of any threatening connotations. It is my impression, from the historians I have read, that up until the point in the sixteenth century when the dominant classes began to change their relationship to popular culture, they not only participated in it, but did so knowingly. They were not, in other words, like tourists who observe or even participate in the rituals of some exotic, "primitive" (but clearly foreign, other) tribe without being aware of the meaning of those rituals. Rather, they were like members of a neighboring tribe, which has its own rituals, its own culture, but which is nonetheless very familiar with, and understands full well the significance of, the culture of its neighbors. While the dominant classes may not have regarded the antagonistic aspects of popular culture as a serious threat, I do not believe that they failed to perceive this antagonism, this hostility toward themselves. Hence, when Rabelais included some of these antagonistic aspects in *Pantagruel* (Epistemon's description of Hell, the humiliation of the "great lady of Paris," etc.), I do not believe that he was in any sense defusing or sanitizing the culture of which they were a part. Unlike Bakhtin, I do not believe that their presence in Rabelais's narrative necessarily argues for an equal hostility on the part of the author; neither do I believe that Rabelais "cleansed" them of their antagonism by including them in his novel. When he uses popular culture in his narrative, Rabelais seems perfectly willing to preserve its social antagonism; rather than defuse or sanitize it later, when this culture is no longer so readily accepted by his potential readers, he excluded it from his texts.

But what then, one might ask, were Rabelais's intentions in including popular culture in his first narrative? They cannot easily be explained as a desire to express an antiestablishment view congruent with certain aspects of that culture itself. In other words, I do not believe that Rabelais was writing from the point of view of the people. Neither, however, would I feel comfortable dismissing the question with talk of "aesthetic preoccupations," something to the effect that Rabelais employed popular culture in *Pantagruel* without regard to its sociocritical aspect because he found it necessary to achieve his artistic goals. He may well have found popular culture artistically useful, but I do not believe that he employed it without regard for its sociocritical significance.

Nor did it simply "come with the territory," so that Rabelais could be described as having used it unthinkingly as a given. As I have already mentioned (n. 43 in the preceding section), Rabelais's primary "source" for *Pantagruel*, the *Great and Inestimable Chronicles*, is almost entirely devoid of popular culture. If this culture is present in Rabelais's first narrative, it is because Rabelais willfully included it, added it to the already established world of Gargantua. But why?

Before this question can be answered properly, the distinctions I have drawn between "learned" and "popular" culture need to be blurred somewhat—though only somewhat. Gérard Defaux reminded me, quite rightly, that Rabelais and his educated contemporaries were very familiar with a part of classical literary tradition that, following Lucian, Horace, Juvenal, Martial, and others, included references to sex, excrement, and "the material bodily lower stratum" in its otherwise quite learned discourse. Bakhtin might well have argued that such classical writers derived these elements of their works from contemporary popular culture, and he most probably would have been right, but the fact remains that these elements would have been perceived by Rabelais and his contemporaries as pertaining to and part of learned as much as popular tradition. As examples of this point, Defaux cited two very learned—indeed, Latin—texts largely contemporary with *Pantagruel*: Erasmus's *Praise of Folly* (1511) and the anonymous *Letters of Obscure Men* (1515).

Defaux's reminder is an important one, because it makes clear that what Bakhtin—and I—have categorized as the "popular culture" aspect of *Pantagruel* is actually a "complex phenomenon" (to use Defaux's own term). Since Rabelais's readers would have been familiar with this—what Defaux calls the "*ridentem dicere verum*" aspect of classical discourse—one must ask to what extent they and Rabelais himself would have seen *Pantagruel* as containing popular, in the sense of "nonlearned," culture.

In response, several observations can be made. First, and perhaps most importantly, while the *ridentem dicere verum* tradition certainly included references to sex, excrement, and the bodily lower stratum, it did *not* include other elements of what has been described as the popular culture aspect of *Pantagruel*. Most notable is the antiestablishment, inverted-world imagery of the carnival. Similarly, though Erasmus and the author(s) of the *Letters of Obscure Men* included "references to sex, excrement, etc." in their learned literary work and used these references, in part, in their attacks on such establishment institutions as the Catholic church and the great universities, nevertheless these authors and their works never suggested any serious criticism of the basic, nonegalitarian social structure.

Two passages from Erasmus are worth citing on this point. In his letter to Martin Dorp, written in 1515 to defend *The Praise of Folly* and subsequently often printed as an appendix to that work, Erasmus asserted: "I carefully avoided writing anything . . . prejudicial to civil order" (156; *OE* 2:102). In a *Colloquy* that

Erasmus published in March 1529, the character Petronius complains: "It's amazing that princes, whose duty it is to look out for the commonwealth, at least in matters pertaining to the person—and in this regard nothing is more important than sound health—don't devise some remedy for this situation [the recent spread of venereal disease]. So huge a plague has filled a large part of the globe—and yet [the princes] go on snoring as if it made no difference at all." Petronius's interlocutor, Gabriel, promptly admonishes: "One must speak guardedly of princes, Petronius," and that is the end of the matter (408–9; 596–97).

Second, it must also be noted that the learned discourse of the early sixteenth century, despite its authors' admiration for the great classical writers, did not embrace the full extent of the *ridentem dicere verum* tradition. Again, Erasmus serves as a convenient illustration. In the "Letter to Thomas More" which he affixed to *The Praise of Folly* as a preface, Erasmus explained that, "unlike Juvenal, I did not stir up that cesspool of secret vice; I took pains to survey funny rather than filthy vices" (5; *ME* 68–69). Some of his readers evidently thought that, even so, he had gone too far in the "references to sex, excrement, etc." that he did include in the text; after the work's early editions, Erasmus felt it necessary to ask Martin Dorp:

Where . . . do you encounter the least bit of filthy or vitriolic language [in the text of *The Praise of Folly*]? Where do I dip into the cesspool of vice? Where do I stir up that hidden, "noisome swamp" of human life? Everyone knows how much could be said against evil popes, wicked bishops and priests, vicious princes, in short, against every rank of society, if (like Juvenal) one were not ashamed to express in writing what many are not ashamed to put into action. All I did was to recount such things as are entertaining and laughable rather than foul. [146; *OE* 2:95–96]

Erasmus returned to this point several times in the course of his epistle: "What I wrote is the truth. . . . It is entertaining rather than obscene" (148; *OE* 2:96–97); "I handle a basically licentious subject with no license" (154; *OE* 2:100–101); "I carefully avoided writing anything obscene or harmful to morals" (156; *OE* 2:102). Even though such aspects of *Pantagruel* as Panurge's suggestion for the fortification of Paris and his story about the old woman, the lion, and the fox might have been readily acceptable to Juvenal, Martial, and Catullus, such more "fanciful" "references to sex, excrement, etc." were no longer part of learned culture by the early sixteenth century.[10]

As I hope the preceding paragraphs have shown, it can safely be said that while some of what Bakhtin (and I) have labeled as "popular culture" in *Pantagruel* may have been perceived by Rabelais and his readers as deriving from learned as much as popular traditions, a substantial amount would have struck Rabelais and his contemporaries as uniquely popular.

With this caveat once made, I can return to my initial question: why did Rabelais add elements—indeed, much of the world view—of popular culture to the already established world of Gargantua? In answer, I would say that I suspect that he included it in *Pantagruel* to take advantage of the self-critical perspective that the dominant classes accepted as long as they were bi-cultural. In this respect, Bakhtin (though he goes to indefensible excesses with his talk of "storming" and "destroying") would seem correct in his interpretation—if, unlike Bakhtin, we limit it to the first narrative. Very much unlike Bakhtin, however, it must be remembered that if Rabelais included such a critique, the dominant classes already accepted the like within their cultural realm. Hence such a critique would not necessarily have been regarded as a commentary from without, the expression of a "foreign" point of view. However important the inclusion of such a judgment might have been to Rabelais, the fact remains that he excluded it from his subsequent narratives when these dominant classes, in restricting their cultural range, changed their relationship to the culture that contained such an external critique. In other words—and here completely in contradiction to Bakhtin—when such a critique began to be perceived as being uniquely the expression of a "foreign" and hostile group, Rabelais ceased to include it in his narratives.

Another possible reason for Rabelais's inclusion of popular culture in *Pantagruel* may have been more aesthetic. If one compares Rabelais's narratives—any of them—to the major works of French prose fiction immediately preceding them (for example, Jean Lemaire de Belges's once highly admired *Illustrations of Gaul and Singularities of Troy*, c. 1512), one is struck immediately by one major stylistic difference. Unlike his predecessors in French literary prose, Rabelais introduced an amazing mixture of styles, tones, and levels of discourse into his works. It is very possible that Rabelais chose to include popular culture in his otherwise establishment, learned discourse as yet another way of bringing about this new stylistic heterogeneity. Still, in calling this a "more aesthetic" reason, I do not wish to suggest that it was altogether divorced from social factors. It is possible that in mixing popular and learned cultures Rabelais thought to appeal to a readership much like himself, professionals (doctors, lawyers, and the like) who certainly participated fully in learned culture and profited from the maintenance of the status quo, but who, since they did not enjoy the wealth and power of the aristocracy and may indeed have envied and even resented it, might have been imagined to delight in certain of the antiestablishment aspects of popular culture.[11]

Even with the depopularization of his second narrative, there is reason to wonder how Rabelais perceived *Gargantua*—or thought others of his world would perceive it—with regard to this point. He would certainly have been expected to dedicate a work to his new patron, Jean du Bellay; yet when he did so, shortly after his return from Rome, he chose not *Gargantua*, but his edition of Marliani's *Typographia Antiquae Romae*. Here it would help greatly to know more precisely the date of *Gargantua*'s first publication. If it was not ready for the printers until sometime in 1535, one can understand that Rabelais might have chosen to dedicate the *Typographia* to du Bellay because he wanted to present the bishop with an offering as soon as possible after his return from Italy. On the other hand, if he published *Gargantua* as early as 1534, as some scholars have argued, one might wonder whether the choice of the *Typographia* indicates that Rabelais felt *Gargantua* was still not altogether of a sort to please a distinguished member of the "new" nobility. (Rabelais evidently did feel able to offer the members of his new world his third and fourth narratives: the *Third Book* is prefaced by a dedicatory poem to Margaret of Navarre, Francis I's sister, and the *Fourth Book* appears with a dedicatory epistle to Odet de Coligny, cardinal of Chastillon, a member of one of France's great noble families. As will be demonstrated later, those works are even more removed from popular culture than *Gargantua*.)

The second new world that Rabelais encountered during his trip to Italy was Italy itself. Nor, perhaps, was this encounter merely an incidental, if fortuitous, benefit of the writer's recent association with du Bellay. In the dedicatory epistle for his edition of the *Typographia Antiquae Romae*, Rabelais assures the bishop that his greatest desire ever since he had become acquainted with "polished letters" had been to travel through Italy and see Rome, "the capital of the world."[12] If true—and it certainly fits with what little we know about Rabelais at this time—it is possible that Rabelais might have sought out du Bellay, hearing that the latter was going to Rome (and perhaps even that he was ill), and offered his medical services in order to be allowed a chance to realize that desire which "he had most desired to fulfill ever since he had first come into contact with polished letters."

Given Rabelais's long-standing fascination with and desire to visit Italy, it is not difficult to imagine that he might have been profoundly affected by a journey to "the land where the lemon-trees bloom." He was not the first, nor certainly the last, northern European to be so affected. In this instance, however, the potential influence of the Italian peninsula was enhanced by the lively intellectual life to be encountered there during the early sixteenth century, as well as the apparently advanced state of learned, court culture—advanced, at least, over what was to be found in France, even at the court of Francis I, much less in the regional circles of provincial French noblemen and scholars such as d'Estissac and Tiraqueau. Though the change in the views and life-style of the elite was gradual in any one place, because Italy was ahead of France on this point (and remained so until at least the middle of the century), a journey from France to Italy during the first half of the century would have brought home to a Frenchman all the more sharply the changes under way in Europe's learned culture.

To begin with, Rabelais almost certainly would have encountered Baldassare Castiglione's *Il Cortigiano*, or at least talk about it.[13] The work had first appeared six years before, in 1528, and its immediate success, if certainly a tribute to Castiglione's talent as an author, is also an indication that there was a substantial audience in Italy (and, later, elsewhere) that shared the views expressed in the dialogues. Among these views, there is, near the beginning of book 2, a discussion of how the nobleman must keep himself distinct from, not act like or consort as an equal with, the people. No longer should members of the nobility engage in wrestling matches and other such contests with peasants, messer Federico says, adding: "It is too unseemly and too ugly a thing, and quite without dignity, to see a gentleman defeated by a peasant" (101; 104). No longer should nobles include peasants in their displays of military prowess (104; 106–7). The ideal courtier must now define himself with his own terms, not in relation to a people who are found to be different and degrading.

A similar attitude is to be found in the greatest and most successful literary work to come out of Italy during this period, Ludovico Ariosto's *Orlando furioso* (first published 1516, with the last revision in 1532).[14] Over and over again throughout the work, a very clear distinction is made between Orlando, Ruggiero, and the other knights on the one hand, individuals with merits such as honor and virtue, and the "menial horde" on the other, almost always treated as a mass or mob, and constantly qualified with such disparaging adjectives as "common" (169, 240; 16.23.7, 20.91.6), "ignorant and mindless" (60, 272, 311; 7.2.2, 23.52.5, 26.33.6), and "despised" (456; 38.11.8). Early in the work, Orlando throws Cimosco's proto-firearm into the sea "to ensure that . . . no villain [*rio*] will ever again boast himself the equal of a good man [*buono*, i.e., noble] because of you" (92; 9.90.5–8); later, he disdains concern about an attack by the "menial horde" (125; 12.78.6) and will not engage them in combat.

Just as the people are treated with disdain in this work by both the main characters and the author, so any aspect of popular culture is carefully excluded. There is no talk of excrement (save the one strange episode of Astolfo and the harpies, canto 33), little mention of disease (and certainly none of venereal disease), no use of popular songs or stories or sayings, and almost no mention of sex.[15] Though some of the Italian works in this mock-heroic vein from the preceding century had incorporated such elements, Ariosto created a poem, and a world, that was almost completely divorced from popular culture—and it became a great success with, and indeed something of a textbook for, an audience that was trying to bring about a similar divorce in their own lives.

Burke explained this divorce in part, and without specific reference to Italy, by suggesting that as the nobility's military role declined in the first half of the sixteenth century, they had to find other ways of justifying their privileges (271). This decline of the military role of the nobility was nowhere more evident and sudden than in Italy. Throughout the fifteenth century, the Italian peninsula had been the stage for countless small wars and battles, as the five major powers (Venice, Milan, Florence, Rome, and Naples) and several lesser principalities vied with each other to maintain and increase their territorial holdings. Then almost overnight, with the invasion of the French and the fall of the Medici in 1494, Italian politics was radically altered. From then on, and as the imperial sack of Rome in 1527 made only too evident, the various Italian city-states were deprived of much of their previous power of self-determination. From 1494 on, Italian politics was dominated by outside forces—France and the emperor—either directly (as with the sack of Rome), or indirectly (as with the French influence in Florentine politics). As a result, and unlike in previous centuries, during the first part of the sixteenth century military prowess was no longer a major way for the Italian noble to demonstrate his superiority, and thereby justify his privileges, because opportunities to display such prowess became far rarer.

This may, in part, explain another way in which the elite, learned culture began to distinguish itself from the people at this time: the upper classes became less tolerant of violence. In *The Civilizing Process*, unquestionably one of the most fascinating books dealing with changes in manners from the Middle Ages to the sixteenth century, Norbert Elias demonstrates how the "secular upper class" progressively devalued aggressiveness and violence at this time.[16] During the Middle Ages, as he shows, restraint in one's interpersonal actions was far less developed than it is today. All levels of men—peasants, bourgeois, nobles— gave vent to their feelings in violently aggressive acts far more freely. With the coming of the Renaissance, and beginning at the top of the social structure with the secular upper class, such impulsive, violent aggression was more and more condemned, the social tolerance of such behavior progressively lessened.

Such a condemnation may have been brought about, in part, by the changing role of the nobility. As the nobles found themselves with less and less opportunity to engage in warfare, to prove and justify themselves in combat, and an increasing amount of time to be spent at court, where one was judged by one's ability to coexist with others rather than to defeat or kill them, there was every need to condemn the violent expression of emotions that had been so much more "useful" in previous centuries.

This is certainly not to suggest that there was the development of anything like our modern pacifist mentality. The nobility still prized tournaments and other opportunities to display their command of the "chivalric" martial arts. Castiglione's locutors emphasize the importance for the ideal courtier of being able to shine in such exercises (32–39; 36–44); Ariosto's heroes—and heroines—delight in nothing else half as much. Indeed, Henry II of France was particularly fond of such activity and met his death in 1559 as the result of his participation in a tourney. Yet a very definite distinction was now being made between chivalric prowess and combat on the one hand (such as jousting between knights who followed all the rules), and the violently aggressive expression of emotion (unrestricted by chivalric forms) on the other. Using the *Orlando furioso* as a source of examples, one could cite the repeated contrast between the "mindless rabble" that is always attacking like a mob, as if in a rage, without apparent reason or form, and the knights, who disdain such "tactics," and fight only in a manner that will allow them to earn honor from a victory, that is, when they engage their opponent in a fair fight carried out according to the accepted chivalric rules.[17]

This change of upper-class views on the acceptability of violent, unregulated aggression can also be seen reflected in the change from *Pantagruel* to *Gargantua*. Rabelais's first narrative contains a great deal of very violent, extraconventional behavior, which seldom carries any condemnation. Panurge's opening story, concerning his escape from the Turks, demonstrates an almost joyous aggressiveness, such as Elias shows to have been typical of the Middle Ages. Pantagruel's new companion recounts as entertainment to his listeners how he set fire to his guard and skewered his guard's master with a spit (215, 216; *P* 77, 79); his audience seems to be quite amused and by no means shocked or horrified. The chapters devoted to detailing Panurge's "Character and Qualities" include descriptions of how he attacked the Paris night patrol by rolling a wagon at them (222; *P* 90) and by sprinkling the streets with gunpowder which he ignited when they marched by (223; *P* 90–91), and of how he burned men and women at church using a magnifying glass (224; *P* 92–93). Later, during the war against the Dipsodes, Panurge trips up and sets fire to 659 Dipsodian cavalrymen with gleeful enjoyment (249–50; *P* 134).

The narrative's title character is, if anything, even more given to violence. From the very moment of his birth, Pantagruel is destructive: he causes his mother's death in the process of being born, "for he was so amazingly large and so heavy that he could not come into the world without suffocating his mother" (174; *P* 17). Subsequently, the infant giant devours one of the cows that nurse him, seeming to delight in its screams as he pulls it apart limb by limb (179; *P* 24). He rips to pieces one of his father's pet bears (179–80; *P* 25) and breaks his cradle "into more than five hundred thousand pieces with a blow of his fist, which he struck at the middle of it in his rage, swearing that he would never go back into it" (181; *P* 26).

Nor is this aggression simply an exaggerated portrayal of "normal" childhood behavior. While Pantagruel, by now an adult, is studying in Valence, several hooligans try to prevent another student from joining in a public dance. "Seeing this, Pantagruel pursued them with a rain of blows as far as the banks of the Rhone, and would have made them all drown, had they not hidden underground like moles a good mile and a half under the water" (182–83; *P* 30). When the student from Limoges continues to speak in his absurdly Latinized French despite Pantagruel's protests, Pantagruel seizes him by the throat and begins to throttle him (185; *P* 34). Addressing Baisecul before the latter's dispute with Humevesne, Pantagruel warns him: "Stick to the truth. For, so help me God, if you tell so much as one word of a lie I'll strike your head from off your shoulders" (205; *P* 60). Entering the hall for Panurge's debate with Thaumaste, Pantagruel shouts at the crowd: "Peace, in the devil's name, peace! By God, you rogues, if you disturb me here with your noise I'll cut off the heads of every one of you" (233; *P* 107–8). Having killed Loupgarou in one-on-one combat, Pantagruel grabs the corpse by the feet and proceeds to swing it around like a scythe, massacring all the other enemy giants in the process (264; *P* 157). As all these examples should make quite clear, violent, un-regulated aggression is by no means excluded from *Pantagruel*, and is even a major trait of the title character, himself a prince.

Again, and not surprisingly, all this changes with *Gargantua*. Despite his abnormal way of issuing from his mother's womb, Gargantua, unlike Pantagruel, seems to cause his mother no un-due discomfort in the process of being born (chap. 6). Though he is also nursed by cows, he, unlike Pantagruel, does them no harm (53; *G* 54), nor does he in any way during his childhood and adolescence demonstrate anything even vaguely reminis-cent of young Pantagruel's destructive behavior.[18] The closest he comes to such violence—and to enjoyment of violence—is his reaction to his mare's demolition of the forest of Beauce with her tail: "At the sight of this Gargantua felt very great delight" (73; *G* 105). Even here, it should be noted, it is only trees, and not men or even animals, that are destroyed.

During the war that comprises the second half of the nar-rative, Gargantua does engage in more violence. He demolishes a chateau held by the enemy with a large treetrunk, and "those inside were all crushed and smashed to pieces" (118; *G* 210); he follows Picrochole's fleeing army after their final defeat, "killing and massacring" (144; *G* 269). One might note, however, that in one episode Rabelais is careful to keep his protagonist from re-peating a violent interpersonal act committed by the "original" Gargantua. In the *Grandes et inestimables cronicques*, 205 individ-uals wander by mistake into Gargantua's mouth while he is sleeping. When the giant awakes, he drinks a riverful of water; "then all the citizens who had fallen into his mouth were drowned" (124). In *Gargantua*, six pilgrims end up inside Gar-gantua's mouth, and the giant subsequently takes "a huge gulp of strong white wine" (121; *G* 218). "The torrent of wine almost carried them down into the abyss of his stomach," the narrator admits, but they take shelter behind Gargantua's teeth, and so are able to survive the deluge.

Yet another development which Rabelais would have encoun-tered in Italy—though one whose influence on him is much more difficult to assess—was a lively discussion about the proper Italian for literary and courtly discourse, "la questione della lingua." The vernacular tongue which has evolved into modern standard Italian made a glorious literary debut in the late thirteenth and early fourteenth centuries at the hands of such giants as Dante, Petrarch, and Boccaccio, but by the fifteenth century it had gone into decline as a literary language. Caught up in the fevered excitement that accompanied the rediscovery of classical Latin texts, most Italian writers of the fifteenth century abandoned their native tongue as a medium of important literary discourse and turned more and more exclusively to Latin. When this trend was reversed in the early sixteenth century, Italian writers found themselves confronted with a major problem: they no longer had at their disposal a living, contemporary literary Italian. The vernacular employed by the fourteenth-century masters (principally Boccaccio and Petrarch), though the object of much praise and admiration, seemed to many unacceptably old-fashioned and hence ridiculous.

As a result, several possible solutions were proposed, often in discussions among courtiers such as those idealized by Castiglione. Some Italians, such as Romolo Amaseo, supported a continued use of Latin, on the grounds that it was the language of gentlemen whereas the vernacular was the speech of the lower classes. "A language of the plebs is a plebian language," wrote the humanist Francesco Bellafini in 1530.[19] Unlike the debate in France several decades later, however, the language debate in Italy did not generally center on whether the vernacular was as deserving as Latin to be used in serious intellectual and literary discourse; most of the disputants were willing to accept it as a medium capable of expressing elevated thought and great artistic inspiration. The argument, instead, revolved around what type of Italian was to be employed. Mario Equicola (d. 1525), a learned courtier and secretary to the marchesana of Mantua, proposed that writers should draw upon the most cultivated usage at the papal court, and considered the living Tuscan dialect to be a plebian language. "As in political life, so also in speaking," he wrote, "we should distinguish ourselves in some fashion from the ignorant multitude." Castiglione's principal speaker on this topic, Count Ludovico da Canossa, proposes much the same solution: literary and spoken Italian should be derived from the best of what was currently spoken at the various princely courts (cf. 47–64; 51–69). Others, such as the humanist and poet Pietro Bembo (who figures as one of the locutors in Castiglione's dialogues, though his real-life position is advanced not by the character with his name but by Federico Fregoso), argued in favor of continued usage of the Italian of Petrarch and Boccaccio, despite the obsolescence of some of its vocabulary and forms. (In his *Prose della volgar lingua*, completed c. 1512, Bembo criticized Dante for using "crude, filthy, ugly, and very harsh" words.) Still others, mostly Tuscans, maintained that the contemporary Tuscan dialect should be the language of choice, claiming that it was the direct—and improved—descendant of the language of the fourteenth-century masters. Eventually it was Bembo's viewpoint that won out, but as is quite evident, "in this debate, it was impossible to obfuscate the social core of the question."[20]

Discussions concerning the choice of a literary and philosophical language did not really get under way in France until the middle of the sixteenth century, and then they had a somewhat different focus, being devoted less to choosing what kind of French was best and more to defending the claims of the French language to be a medium worthy and capable of conveying great literature.[21] Rabelais, who wrote most of his works before this discussion began, did not publish anything that we still possess or know of on this question.[22] Still, one can hazard certain cautious observations on apparent differences between *Pantagruel* and *Gargantua* along these lines.

First, let it be said quite categorically that Rabelais never excluded popular language from his narratives. The chronologically second (*Gargantua*), *Third*, and *Fourth Books* all contain terms—and not simply euphemisms—for the various bodily excretions, the sexual organs, the sexual act, and so on.[23] But there do appear to be certain changes. In *Pantagruel*, in an episode that has already been the object of perhaps too much modern critical attention, Pantagruel and his companions meet a student from Limoges who insists upon speaking an almost incomprehensible mixture of French and bad Latin, which he seems to believe will cause him to be taken for a Parisian university student. After several times expressing his impatience with this linguistic pretentiousness, Pantagruel picks up the Limousin by the throat and proceeds to throttle him. Terrified (and no doubt in considerable pain), the student reverts to his native *patois*, hearing which, Pantagruel exclaims, "Now you're speaking naturally" (185; *P* 34). The narrator concludes this chapter by saying that the Limousin's fate (he eventually died) proves that "we ought to speak the language in common use" (185; *P* 35). Though by "the language in common use" (*le langaige usité*), Rabelais certainly means, in part, a living, "natural" language, as opposed to an artificial tongue contrived by students—"as Caesar [Augustus] said, we should shun absurd words as carefully as ships' pilots avoid the rocks at sea" (ibid.)²⁴—he also seems to recommend the language in common use, that in use by everyone. There is no distinction made between different levels or class affiliations.

This one line is not very much to build on for *Pantagruel*, but in *Gargantua* there are no direct comments about proper language. There is still a great deal of popular discourse in the second narrative, albeit perhaps not as much as in the first and not so evenly distributed among all the characters (the mature Gargantua's language is far less "popular" than Friar John's, for instance). But, more than in the first work, there is in the second a definite display of a more formal, learned discourse. *Pantagruel* has the letter from Gargantua to his son (chap. 8), perhaps the most often excerpted passage in Rabelais's entire opus. As is appropriate to its subject matter—Gargantua is trying to convince his son of the importance of education—the epistle is couched in a very formal, indeed highly Latinate, style.

Still, this piece, however famous, is really the only one of its kind in Rabelais's first narrative. Such language becomes more prominent as of *Gargantua*. The most obvious instance is Ulrich Gallet's speech to Picrochole (chap. 31), an example of almost Ciceronian rhetorical eloquence in French.²⁵ But there is also Gargantua's speech to the vanquished Lernean troops (chap. 50) and, to an extent, the concluding description of the Abbey of Theleme (chaps. 53–57). What was coming to be seen as "popular language" is not excluded from *Gargantua*—as some of the Italians mentioned above were advocating for literature, its learned authors, and its learned and courtly readers—but the second narrative does contain more examples of learned (and totally "folk-free") discourse.

This last point is directly related to another possible explanation of why Rabelais chose to exclude, or at least drastically play down, popular culture in his works as of *Gargantua*. It would appear that *Pantagruel* had not been taken seriously by readers when it first appeared. In 1533, a minor Neo-Latin poet, Nicolas Bourbon, published the following epigram in his *Nugae*:

> In mentem tibi quid, Rabelle, venit
> Nostros discipulos ut avocare
> Nusquam a munere desinas honesto
> Nimirum a studio politiorum
> Sacrarumque ab amore literarum?
> Malles quippe tuis in salebris,
> In nugis hominum tenebricosis,
> In tricisque librisque quaestuosis,
> Foeda in barbarie, in fimo inque coeno
> Tam bonam male perderent iuventam:
> Atqui (si mihi credis) ipse, posthac
> Nostros discipulos sines valere,
> Ne quas persequeris furens ubique,
> Te ludos faciant in orbe Musae,
> Ac ne te in rabiem inferant Rabelle.[26]

(What came into your mind, Rabelais, that you called our students to desist from honest work, from the study of "polished," and the love of sacred, letters? Do you prefer that they lose such fine youth in [the reading of] your rough things, in the dark trifles of men, in nonsense and in books written for profit, in barbaric filth, in dung and in mud? And if you believe me, henceforth you should let our students do something worthwhile, unless you want to be chased everywhere and have tricks played on you by the angry Muses, and unless you want them to drive you into a rage.)

Bourbon sees the reading of *Pantagruel* as the opposite of the "study of 'polished' letters," since he accuses Rabelais of having drawn students away from the latter by providing them with the former. Furthermore, in describing *Pantagruel* as "sale-brae" (rough, uneven), "nugae" (trifles, nonsense), "tricae" (like "nugae"), "foedus," "fimus," and "caenum" (all synonyms for mud, filth, dung, etc.), Bourbon seems to deny the work any importance or value.

Of course, Bourbon's judgment may not have been altogether unbiased. As a Neo-Latin poet, he was one of a now completely forgotten (and even then, not particularly well-known) group of writers who lived in perpetual penury because then (as now) there was no market for works such as theirs.[27] *Pantagruel*, on the other hand, seems to have sold quite well, from the very beginning. Since Bourbon condemns Rabelais's work not only for containing "mere trifles" and "filth," but also for being "libri quaestuosi" (profit-making books), it is quite possible that Bourbon, like many commercially unsuccessful writers before and since, portrayed *Pantagruel* as necessarily without value because it appealed to the "masses" (if one can use such a term in speaking of the sixteenth-century book-buying public), "masses" which, since they failed to appreciate his own, obviously worthwhile efforts, were not in Bourbon's opinion capable of discerning the merit of truly fine literature.

Nevertheless, it would appear that Bourbon's evaluation of *Pantagruel* was shared by others, readers from whom Rabelais evidently expected a more perceptive judgment. In the Prologue to *Gargantua*, he wrote:

You, my good disciples and other learned fools, in reading the pleasant titles of certain books of our invention, such as *Gargantua*, *Pantagruel* . . . too easily conclude that they treat of nothing but mockery, fooling, and pleasant fictions [*menteries*], seeing that their outward signs—their titles, that is—are commonly greeted, without further investigation, with smiles of derision. It is wrong, however, to set such small store by the works of men. . . . You must open this book, and carefully weigh up its contents. You will discover then that the drug within is far more valuable than the box promised; that is to say, that the subjects here treated are not so foolish as the title on the cover suggests. [37–38; *G* 11–12]

Rabelais then goes on to develop this point with the famous metaphor of the "substantial marrow" (38; *G* 12–14).[28] As Gérard Defaux has demonstrated in *Pantagruel et les sophistes*, there is indeed a good deal more to *Pantagruel* than "mockery, fooling, and pleasant fictions"; if that is how his first novel was received, Rabelais would certainly have had good reason to be disappointed.

In fact, the reception accorded his initial effort may have been another trigger, along with the journey to Italy, that caused Rabelais himself to begin to reject popular culture: after having included it so abundantly in *Pantagruel* and then having seen how a work containing popular culture was greeted, Rabelais may have had brought home to him for the first time in a very personal, direct way that the participants in learned culture, his intended audience, were abandoning and denigrating the traditions which they, and certainly their forbears, had so wholeheartedly embraced.[29]

Yet another explanation for the change from *Pantagruel* to *Gargantua* that is specific, or at least somewhat specific, to Rabelais involves still another difference between the two novels. *Gargantua* is strongly differentiated from *Pantagruel* by the characterization (or "motivation") of the enemy that invades Utopie in the second half of the two novels. In *Pantagruel*, Anarche and the Dipsodians are presented much like any invaders of adventure fiction; almost no attention is paid to the motivation or reason behind their attack. In *Gargantua*, on the other hand, the enemy invasion is presented as a serious, dangerous affair. It is suggested that Satan has seized hold of part of humanity (the Lerneans) in order to destroy the rest of it. When Grandgousier is first informed of Picrochole's invasion of Utopie, he exclaims: "It must be the evil spirit [*l'esprit maling*, i.e., Satan] that has prompted him to outrage me now" (102; *G* 177–78). Later, near the end of his address to Picrochole, Ulrich Gallet tells the King of Lerné that "if the spirit of slander [*l'esperit calumniateur*, another term for Satan], striving to induce you to evil, had by deceitful appearances and fallacious visions put it into your head that we had acted towards you in any way unworthy of our ancient friendship, you should first have inquired into the truth of the matter and then have given us warning. We should then have acted so completely to your satisfaction that you would have had occasion to be pleased" (106; *G* 187). From these two passages it is clear that both Grandgousier and Ulrich Gallet believe (and Rabelais, offering no contradiction or other explanation, wants his readers to believe) that the cause of Picrochole's actions is more than simply an imbalance of the four humours within his system—that is, a dominance of the choleric humour, or bile (hence his name, "Picro*chole*"), over the other three. The impetus behind his unprovoked violence lies, it is concluded, with the Prince of Darkness himself.[30]

Rabelais, in response, seems to pare his heroes (the Utopians) down to fighting trim in order to emphasize the qualities that he felt to be necessary for those faced with such a formidable opponent. Whereas in *Pantagruel* both Anarche and Pantagruel had been accused of madness (*folie*) (257, 264; *P* 145, 156) and both the Dipsodian and the Utopian soldiers depicted as disorderly (258, 253; *P* 147, 138), in *Gargantua*, Rabelais excludes *folie* from the presentation of his heroes, and the Utopians are consistently—and exclusively—associated with reason (102, 103; *G* 178, 181)[31] and order (141; *G* 263–64). *Folie/fureur*, excess, and disorder are now all the exclusive attributes of the "bad guys," the Lerneans. One is therefore tempted to suggest that Rabelais brought about the exclusion of popular culture from his second work because he felt that such traits would weaken men's ability to withstand and overcome a challenge that he had not seen his men—or men in general—facing as of 1532.

The change in the presentation of the warring armies is accompanied by the exclusion of sexual desire from the source of power and authority in the second novel. As has already been shown, the character in *Pantagruel* who is far and away the most preoccupied and occupied with sex is Panurge. But this "sex maniac" is also a leader, someone who very much occupies the locus of power. In *Pantagruel et les sophistes*, Defaux has demonstrated how Panurge throughout the novel increasingly comes to assume much of the authority first held by Pantagruel. Nowhere is this more evident than in the section devoted to the Utopie-Dipsodie war. It is Panurge who engineers the death of all but one of the 660 cavalrymen who ride against Pantagruel's army as they first land in Utopie (249–50; *P* 132–34), Panurge who recalls the others (including Pantagruel) to planning the forthcoming battle when these others become too concerned with eating (252; *P* 136), Panurge who has Pantagruel consume great quantities of wine and then certain drugs so that the giant will flood the enemy camp with his urine (258–60; *P* 147–50), Panurge who urges Pantagruel on against the Dipsodian giants when the Utopian prince hesitates (261–62; *P* 151–52), Panurge who revives Epistemon when the teacher's head is severed from his body during the fighting (264–65; *P* 158–59). It comes as no surprise when Pantagruel, at a difficult moment during his fight with Loupgarou, cries: "Ho, Panurge, where are you?" (263; *P* 156). Given the centrality of Panurge in *Pantagruel*, it becomes clear that, in this novel there is no separation of sexual drive from power and authority, no notion that the former must be excluded from the latter.

By contrast, in the second novel the adult Gargantua is presented as having absolutely no interest in sex. As a result, in *Gargantua* sexual drive is completely excluded from the locus of power and authority, of which the bachelor Gargantua and his aged father (now a widower) are the sole occupants. What little mention of sex there is in the military section of Rabelais's second narrative comes, as already mentioned, from Friar John, a character who, unlike the Panurge of *Pantagruel*, never occupies a position of authority with the protagonist.

The absence of sex and human sexual impulses from the locus of power in *Gargantua* definitely seems to reinforce my interpretation of the differences between *Pantagruel* and *Gargantua* concerning the presentation of the warring armies. Again, it would appear to be a case of "stripping down" in order to be in readiness for the serious conflict ahead. Throughout Western learned thought, sex and sexual impulses have been seen as something that undermines one's strength for other actions. Even in *Pantagruel* the title character makes such a remark, warning his men as they fantasize about what they will do when they capture the prostitutes who accompany Anarche's troops: "You're reckoning without your enemy. . . . I'm very much afraid that before night falls I may see you in such a state that you'll have no great desire to rise. You are more likely to be layed with great blows of the pike and lance" (253; *P* 139).

Sexual drive not only weakens man's strength for other undertakings; it also leads to disorder (and hence to confusion with an enemy that is portrayed as the essence of disorder). Again, there is no need to turn to general Western thought for substantiation of such a commonplace. Certainly nothing illustrates more clearly than the Panurge of *Pantagruel* how a human's sexual impulses can produce disorder. If sex is excluded from the locus of power and authority in *Gargantua*, it would certainly seem to be in part to illustrate how men must prepare themselves for the decisive combat that they are depicted as facing. These men must deny a part of themselves in order to conserve their strength to fight—and avoid becoming confused with—the new, great enemy.

Another difference already noted between *Pantagruel* and *Gargantua* also seems to relate to this preparation for combat. During the construction of the Abbey of Theleme, a blade is found on which is prophesied an era when "[there] will be so many quarrels, / So many discords, so much to and fro, / That history, mighty wonders though it tells, / Has no record of like disturbances" (161; *G* 308). It is as if to make sure that the inhabitants of Theleme are suited to prevail in such a conflict that Rabelais has written over the entrance: "Enter not here . . . you with your sores, gnawed to the bone by pox; / Take your ulcers elsewhere and show them to others, / Scabby from head to toe and brimful of dishonour" (154; *G* 291). In Theleme the residents can say: "Our limbs are sound and strong. / This blessing fills us quite, / Grace, honour, praise, and light" (ibid.). From the society that is being prepared for the upcoming terrible struggle, all manifestations of the unhealthy, all the unsound of body, are carefully excluded.

It becomes very tempting to suggest that, as of *Gargantua*, Rabelais saw certain aspects of popular culture to be dangerous because they could weaken those who would be charged with repelling the attack of Satan. Beginning with chapter 13 in *Gargantua*, Rabelais separates the general discourse of *Pantagruel* (which had included *folie/fureur*, excess, disorder, sex, and the unclean, as well as their opposites) into establishment and nonestablishment discourses. If he allows the nonestablishment discourse to remain present, at a reduced and restricted level, it is henceforth excluded from the privileged locus of power and authority, never given the chance to defame or defile or, more accurately, weaken those in command. These leaders must be kept strong so that they can defend human society against the assaults of the "evil spirit." Rabelais never seems to link such assaults to popular culture, to accuse practitioners of the latter of being in cahoots with Satan,[32] but it seems clear that he regarded certain aspects of popular culture—and primarily sexual license—as weakening and hence dangerous at a time when the leaders of men could not afford to be weak.[33]

Such are some of the possible historical stimuli that may have led Rabelais to reduce the usage of popular culture in his narratives as of *Gargantua*. If the reader accepts my demonstration of this reduction, and my explanations for it, he or she will certainly want to know whether the changes attributed to *Gargantua* were maintained in Rabelais's subsequent narratives.

3

The *Third* and *Fourth Books:*
Continuing the Exclusion

The first edition of *The Third Book of the Heroic Deeds and Sayings of the Good Pantagruel* was brought out by the Parisian publisher Chrestien Wechel in 1546. The work continues the rejection and exclusion of popular culture noted in the second half of *Gargantua*, as well as the greater display of learned culture demonstrated in the second narrative.

The continued distancing from popular culture can be seen even before one gets into the text itself. To begin with, there is the change in publishers. Chrestien Wechel was an editor of distinguished scholarly works, unlike Claude Nourry and François Juste, the publishers of *Pantagruel* and *Gargantua*, who printed many popular *romans de chevalerie*, prose simplifications of the great medieval epics. The move from the two earlier publishers to Wechel would suggest, again, that Rabelais had discovered that an association with popular culture caused his fictional narratives not to be taken seriously by the learned figures for whom he was writing. Wechel's name, on the other hand, would have conveyed an impression of serious, important content.

Much the same would have been suggested by the liminary *dizain*, a poem written to Francis I's very learned and pious sister, Margaret of Navarre:

> Abstracted soul, ravished in ecstasy,
> Returned now to thy home, the Firmament,
> Leaving thy body, formed in harmony,
> Thy host and servant, once obedient

To thy commands in this life transient.
Wouldst thou not care to quit, just fleeting,
Thy heavenly mansion and perpetual,
And here below for the third time to see
The jovial deeds of good Pantagruel?
[280; *TL* 2]

Today Margaret is best remembered for a collection of stories in the style of Boccaccio known as the *Heptameron*. The work was not published until after her death in 1549, however, so in 1546 her name would have been associated primarily with her devout religious poetry and her involvement with a circle of nonpopular religious reformers, the "évangéliques." Though Rabelais's *dizain* is not quite a dedication, it does suggest that the following narrative would be suitable reading for so learned and noble a person as the queen.

Finally, this is the first of the narratives that Rabelais signed with his own name and title: Doctor of Medicine. (The first two narratives have as their author the anagrammatic Alcofribas Nasier.) Such a change can easily be interpreted in a variety of ways, of course, but one that should be readily acceptable is that, in putting his own name on the *Third Book*, Rabelais was cutting down on an earlier element of playfulness. Again, as with the move to Wechel and the poem to Margaret of Navarre, Rabelais's abandonment of a comical pen name suggests a greater seriousness.[1]

One must not stop at the outward signs, however (to paraphrase Rabelais somewhat), but rather, must open the *Third Book* and carefully weigh its contents. When one does so, in the context of the preceding analysis of *Pantagruel* and *Gargantua*, one is struck first by the very considerable augmentation of references to antiquity. This is true not simply of the narrator, but of all the principal characters. Pantagruel certainly leads the way. He cites enough names from classical literature, history, and mythology to have given editors the shivers for centuries afterward. Panurge is not far behind, however. Certain critics' attempts to draw some sort of opposition between the two along the lines of written versus oral culture are, at best, misleading. Though he may not bring into his discourse quite as many literary or historical classical figures as his master, Panurge still fills his speech with enough references to antiquity to make it quite clear that he is a bona fide participant in learned culture, someone well schooled in dominant-class learning.

If, on the one hand, references to antiquity, that sine qua non of Renaissance learned culture, were greatly increased as of the *Third Book*, uses of popular culture, already severely curtailed as of the second half of *Gargantua*, continue to be cut back in Rabelais's third narrative. The *Third Book* contains almost no scenes parallel with passages in the previous narratives to facilitate comparisons, as had been the case between *Gargantua* and *Pantagruel*, but the continued reduction is still not difficult to measure. To begin with, there is almost no mention of disease or infection in the *Third Book*. The "poxy friends" (*verolés*) for whom *Gargantua* was supposedly written (37; *G* 9) have been replaced by "gouty sirs" (*goutteux*) (281; *TL* 7).[2] When sickness is referred to, it has clearly negative connotations. Speaking of potential readers, the narrator says that he does not write for "the breed of pious hypocrites [*Caphars*]"; they are "all scurvy and poxy" [*tous verollez croustelevez*] (286; *TL* 20). Later, when explaining how his father condemned and destroyed a book about using dice to foretell the future, Pantagruel says that Gargantua "completely exterminated, suppressed, and abolished it, as a most dangerous plague" (316; *TL* 87). Similarly, when condemning Panurge's indulgence in debt, Pantagruel remarks: "Let me tell you that if one of your shameless swaggerers and tiresome borrowers were to make a second visit to a city that knew his habits, you would find the citizens more worried and alarmed by his entrance than if the plague had come in person, dressed up as the Tyanian philosopher saw it at Ephesus" (302; *TL* 55). In general, disease is rarely mentioned in the *Third Book*, but when it is included, it is by no means presented as "acceptable," or even "ambivalent."

The same is true of excrement. When it does figure in the third narrative, furthermore, it is only in someone's words, and never, as in the first two works, in its "concrete, visible reality." For example, Friar John mentions that "the Good Fathers of religion," who had been an object of ridicule since *Gargantua*, "on getting up for Matins . . . shat in the shitteries, pissed in the pisseries, [and] spat in the spitteries" (329; *TL* 119). When Panurge is trying to dismiss Raminogrobis and his "prophetic" poem, he accuses the poet of heresy, and foretells that his soul will go "right under Proserpina's close-stool, in the very infernal pot into which she drops the fecal produce of her suppositories" (349; *TL* 161). Similarly, when he becomes upset with Her Trippa, Panurge throws several scatological terms at the necromancer (359; *TL* 184, 185); when he develops a dislike for Rondibilis, he ridicules the doctor with a stercorous Latin distich (384; *TL* 240). In each case, excrement is mentioned only by a nonauthoritative character, and with reference only to others of similar status. In each case, it has not neutral or ambivalent, but strictly negative connotations.[3]

The mention of sex in the *Third Book* is less restricted than that of disease and excrement, which is understandable given that much of the work revolves around the question of marriage—and Panurge's marriage, at that. Still, there is never more than mention of sex; unlike the characters in *Pantagruel* and *Gargantua*, none of those in the *Third Book* ever actually engage in it. And again, like excrement, it is a subject mentioned only by characters outside the locus of power and authority. Panurge tells the story of the deaf mute Verona, who took a young Roman gentleman home to bed with her because she misunderstood his sign language inquiry about directions; it is also he who recounts the more extended tale of Sister Fessue (Fatbum), who so easily acquiesed to the libidinous desires of Brother Royddimet (Stiffcock) (chap. 19). Friar John tells perhaps the most famous such story in the *Third Book*, that of the ring of Hans Carvel (chaps. 26, 28). Pantagruel and Gargantua keep apart from this sort of talk, however. In preparation for the *sortes Virgilianes*, dice are thrown, and the number 16 is obtained. Panurge boasts: "Let the devils look out for themselves, if I don't work on my future wife just that number of times on my wedding night." Pantagruel responds with a reprimand: "There was no need to come out with such a thundering affirmation [*dévotion*]" (316; *TL* 89).[4]

Nothing more clearly indicates the move away from popular culture in the *Third Book* than the treatment of the banquet. When Nazdecabre and Triboullet arrive to be questioned by Panurge, neither is greeted with a dinner. Hippothadée, Rondibilis, and Trouillogan receive better treatment when they convene to counsel the would-be husband, but the resulting banquet certainly is not reminiscent of those in popular culture (or in *Pantagruel*). None of the participants is free with his language or his behavior, not even Panurge, who in this respect bears no resemblance to Friar John in the banquet scene of *Gargantua*. The only slightly off-color remarks made during the dinner—other than Panurge's previously cited distich—occur when several of the participants, following Rondibilis's lead, decide to tell stories about the inferiority of women. All in all, this banquet appears devoid of any similarity to those that figure in popular culture. It is not surprising that when, near the beginning of the novel, Panurge throws "a thousand little banquets and jolly feasts, open to all comers, especially to all who were good company," the *Third Book* narrator mentions this as one of the ways in which Panurge "squandered the whole income of his wardenship" (292; *TL* 28–29).

Other aspects of popular culture found in *Pantagruel* and the early pages of *Gargantua* are altogether absent from the *Third Book*—indeed, replaced by their opposites. The *dolce far niente* positive valuation of idleness associated with the Land of Cockaigne is gone. In the Prologue to the *Third Book*, the narrator compares himself to Diogenes, saying that, just as the Greek philosopher rolled his barrel around Corinth rather than be seen as idle while everyone else was working on the preparations for the defense against Philip of Macedonia, so he is writing this book because "I have felt it to be most disgraceful to stand idly watching. . . . I will not stand by as a useless idler" (283–84; *TL* 13–15).

Nor is there any carnivalesque inversion of social and political hierarchies, or condemnation of those at the top of such power structures. Quite to the contrary, in the first chapter of the *Third Book* the narrator gives a definition of royalty that is the exact opposite of the one put forth by Panurge in *Pantagruel*. Speaking of Hesiod's description of good demons, he says: "And because the riches and favours of heaven come to us from [the good demons'] hands because they are continually doing us good and always preserving us from harm, [Hesiod] says that they are in the position of kings; since always to do good, and never evil, is an act exclusively royal" (290; *TL* 25).

In short, popular culture figures only very occasionally in

the *Third Book*, and in no significant or important—much less threatening—way. One could say much the same thing of its "creator," the people. In the *Third Book*, the characters move in the world of the learned; Panurge consults Vergil's *Aeneid* (in Latin), a poet (Raminogrobis), a learned (if crazy) astrologer (Her Trippa), a theologian (Hippothadée), a physician (Rondibilis), a philosopher (Trouillogan), and a judge (Bridoye). Even the one counselor who would certainly seem to be of the people, the Sibyl of Panzoust,[5] is carefully separated from the relevant aspect of popular culture that was coming to be strongly condemned by the dominant-class establishments. When Pantagruel suggests that Panurge consult the "sibyl" with Epistemon, the pedagogue refuses to go, saying: "Perhaps . . . she is a Canidia, a Sagana, a pythoness, and sorceress [Fr. *sorcière* is also "witch"]. What gives me that idea is that the place has a bad name for sorceresses. There are said to be more there than ever there were in Thessaly. I shouldn't like to go there at all. The thing is wrong." Epistemon's attitude reflects that of the establishments of the time, especially the various organized religions. As of the Late Middle Ages, witchcraft began to be methodically and strenuously condemned and pursued by churches and states.[6] But Pantagruel excludes the possibility of this censured aspect of popular culture altogether from his recommendation of the "sibyl," for he replies to Epistemon's objection: "It is neither verified nor admitted that she is a sorceress. . . . How do we know that she isn't an eleventh sibyl, a Cassandra?" (331; *TL* 123–24). With his choice of words, he returns the "sibyl" to the acceptable, learned realm of antiquity.[7] Even more than in the second half of *Gargantua*, in the *Third Book* popular culture and the people have been almost completely excluded.

Bakhtin mentions no such exclusion. Though he certainly cites the *Third Book* far less than the others, he speaks of the four as a homogeneous, unchanging monolith. Even his critical disciple, Michael Beaujour, acknowledges that there is a difference, however. Though, in *Le jeu de Rabelais* (1969), he accepts Bakhtin's pronouncements on Rabelais and popular culture without question (or independent verification), he does at one point write: "In the *Third Book* . . . the comic becomes mechanical and the book is flooded by Learned discourse [*le discours du*

Savoir]. . . . Carnival is left behind; its clamor falls silent. . . . At the moment of the beginning of the inquiry [Panurge's inquiry about his possible marriage], the *Third* and *Fourth Book*s seem to return to the Humanist fold, abandoning the popular digression."[8] It should be obvious from the preceding pages (or even from a reading of the work itself) that, with the *Third Book*, a major change in *Gargantua and Pantagruel* has taken place, or been reaffirmed. From start to finish, the *Third Book* is a work that could have figured in the library of the Abbey of Theleme, a work written with the values and manners of the second (but not the first) half of *Gargantua*—in other words, the new values and manners of the dominant classes. It is not that Rabelais takes himself and his work more seriously in the *Third Book* than before; I am convinced (as any reader of Defaux and later Screech must be) that Rabelais was quite serious about what he was doing from the opening pages of *Pantagruel*. But I am also convinced that he wanted what he took seriously to be taken equally seriously by his intended readers. After *Pantagruel* and the apparent public reaction to it, he evidently realized that this meant appearing more learned and less "popular" to a public that was beginning to see the popular exclusively as a mark of the lower classes, and hence as having to do with a group that— in the eyes of this public—had nothing "serious" to offer. To the extent that the "popular" was no longer associated with the dominant class—who, in their own eyes, have always been the only group with anything serious or important to say—popular culture was no longer regarded by the upper classes as being likely to express or signal anything of serious import; rather, its presence would more likely have been viewed as an indication of the absence of any such significant content. According to Bakhtin (and Beaujour), Rabelais included aspects of popular culture in his narratives (or, according to Beaujour, in the first two) alongside elements of learned culture in order to ridicule (degrade, contaminate, etc.) the latter by juxtaposition with the former. It would seem to be closer to the truth to say that once Rabelais became aware that the presence of popular culture did in fact degrade or lessen in the eyes of the dominant class that with which it came in contact, he was quick to exclude it from his own works. One can only speculate on the extent to which the author himself shared these shifting values and views. The fact remains, however, that he felt he had something important to say, something he wanted to communicate to certain readers. When he became aware of changes in how these readers judged the important (and unimportant), he made the necessary adjustments in his work to cause it to appear important (and not unimportant) to his chosen public.

This would be all I had to say on the *Third Book* and popular culture, were it not for another "new critic," who has maintained that there is, in fact, an important element of popular culture, or at least of "the people's ideology," in Rabelais's third narrative. While Beaujour was writing his variations on a theme by Bakhtin (in the key of Georges Bataille), Jean Paris, in *Rabelais au futur* (1970), was developing an interpretation of Rabelais drawn from that of Henri Lefebvre (*Rabelais*, 1955).[9] For Paris, the "truth" of *Gargantua and Pantagruel* lay not in its use of popular culture, but rather in its expression of the mentality of the rising middle class. This was a mentality in conflict with itself, according to Paris. On the one hand, he maintained, the middle class in the early sixteenth century looked back to its recently abandoned peasant origins and culture with nostalgia and regret; on the other hand, it gazed up admiringly at the aristocracy, seeking to ape the latter and—so as to gain their acceptance—to deny all links with the former.[10]

Any historian of Early Modern Europe would interrupt right here to protest the notion of a rising middle class in the early sixteenth century.[11] For the sake of argument, however, let us grant the point (if not accept it) so that we can follow Paris in his application of it to the *Third Book*. For Paris, nothing in Rabelais demonstrates this middle-class divided mentality (schizophrenia) better than the opening of the third narrative.[12] In Panurge's uncontrolled spending and squandering of his wardenship of Salmiguondin, and Pantagruel's negative reaction to such extravagance, Paris finds an expression of the rising middle class's nostalgia for its peasant origins and its attempt to adopt a new economic posture. A brief review of chapter 2 is in order.

In the first chapter of the *Third Book*, the narrator describes how Pantagruel gave "order to the government of all Dipsodie" (292; *TL* 28). "Order" would, indeed, seem to reign everywhere in Dipsodie, were it not for Panurge. Having been given the wardenship (*chastellanie*) of Salmiguodin, "the new warden . . . in less than a fortnight . . . squandered the whole income of his wardenship, both fixed and variable, for the next three years" (292–94; *TL* 28–34). He spends his money not for society's benefit ("in such enterprises as founding monasteries, erecting churches," etc.), but in the most disorderly, unrecuperable fashion: "on a thousand little banquets and jolly feasts . . . on felling his timber and burning the great trunks to sell the ashes; on taking money in advance, buying dear, selling cheap, and eating his wheat in the blade." Seeing this, Pantagruel "took Panurge aside, and mildly pointed out to him that if he wished to live in this style and not alter his way of housekeeping, it would be impossible, or at least very difficult, ever to make him rich." Panurge answers that the accumulation of wealth is of no concern to him: "'Rich?' replied Panurge. 'Had you set your heart on that? Did you really mean to make me rich in this world? Set your heart on a merry life, in the name of God and all good men! Don't allow any other care or thought into the sacrosanct domicile of your celestial brain.'" When confronted with the admonition "Thrift! Thrift!" Panurge bursts into laughter, refusing to be caught up in a reasoned husbanding of money and goods. Similarly, he professes an attitude with regard to the future that undermines any motivation for the amassing of capital: "Who can tell whether the world will last another three years? And supposing it were to last longer, is any man such a fool as to dare promise himself three years of life?" As even he is aware, such an ideology is a threat to a developed economic order; by eating his wheat in the blade, he would put all the middlemen in the grain industry out of business: "Eating my wheat in the blade . . . I save the expense of hoers . . . of reapers . . . of gleaners . . . of threshers . . . of millers . . . and of bakers."

Pantagruel perceives the disorder inherent in Panurge's attitude and condemns it soundly as "heresy," a word that never had stronger connotations than during the sixteenth century. He compares Panurge to Nero and Caligula, and finally accuses him of having resurrected the Protervia, a ceremony that "was to the Romans what that of the Paschal lamb was for the Jews. For it entailed eating all that was eatable and throwing the rest in the fire, reserving nothing for the morrow" (295; *TL* 35). The Prince of Utopie then dismisses the whole argument out of hand with a simple "But let that pass" (295; *TL* 36), and the episode—and the chapter—comes to a complete halt.

For Paris, this episode is a clear expression of the "mentality of the rising middle class," with Panurge reflecting a longing for their former "peasant economic ideology" and Pantagruel enforcing a dominant-class, capitalistic economic stance. Paris is circumspect about explaining just why he equates Panurge's views with a peasant, or noncapitalist, system, but some of the adjacent footnotes would seem to suggest that he is making rather oblique reference to a famous work by the French anthropologist Marcel Mauss (and an even more oblique reference to Georges Bataille's essay "La Notion de dépense"). Rather than be equally oblique, let us go back to the source of this interpretation, and I will try to explain how Paris develops it.

At the turn of the century, the American anthropologist Franz Boas undertook a study of certain Pacific North American Indian tribes, among them the Kwakiutl. One of their customs that particularly fascinated him was "potlatch," a ceremony or festivity in which, according to Boas, various chieftains took turns destroying some of their most valued possessions (usually by throwing them into the sea). This squandering of goods was undertaken, in Boas's account, as a form of rivalry, each chieftain trying to outdo the others. Boas's study of potlatch among the Kwakiutl led to monographs on similar customs in other Pacific tribes by anthropologists such as Malinowski and Swanton.

Mauss, here something of an armchair anthropologist, was intrigued by some of these monographs and, without doing any additional fieldwork of his own, wrote a work containing his interpretation of the phenomenon, his "Essai sur le don" (1923).[13] What he actually said, and how he differed from Boas, is not really important for the present discussion. Rather, it bears noting that Mauss's work caught the attention of the French social philosopher Georges Bataille, who reinterpreted these various anthropologists' observations (as presented by Mauss) yet again, this time in the essay "La Notion de dépense" (1933).[14] For Bataille, the lavish destruction of goods by certain Pacific Indian chieftains was a clear manifestation of *dépense* (literally, "expenditure"), what Bataille felt to be the fundamental human need to function outside any closed, recuperative system of economic exchange and reciprocity. In Michèle Richman's words, *dépense*, for Bataille, represented "the 'other' economy: the pull of forces which compel men to gamble, dissipate fortunes, and exhaust great reserves of energy and goods, thus implicitly subverting the hegemony of values which demand productivity, accumulation and concern for the future."[15]

The possible application of all this to chapter 2 of the *Third Book* should be rather obvious. Panurge's squandering of the wardenship of Salmiguondin, his refusal to worry about the future, much less save for it—as well, certainly, as Pantagruel's evocation of the Roman Protervia in speaking of Panurge's behavior—would all make Panurge appear to be a two-legged incarnation of the spirit of *dépense*. Pantagruel's rejection of such economics, his talk about becoming rich and saving for the future, would all make the Prince of Utopie seem to be the quintessential capitalist. If one accepts (as Paris certainly does) Bataille's argument that *dépense* is a "primitive," fundamental aspect of human nature that has been repressed by our modern capitalist ideology, then the Panurge of chapter 2 is clearly the half of the rising middle-class mentality that harks back longingly to its more "primitive," precapitalist self (those good old peasant days, when it was free to indulge in its urge toward *dépense*), while Pantagruel is equally clearly the other half, the part of the middle-class mentality that wants to reject its past and develop a new economic ideology, one in which saving for the future and striving to accumulate wealth are stressed. In other words, Panurge's economics are "popular," whereas Pantagruel's are dominant-class.[16]

There are definite problems with this argument. To begin with, of course, and as already mentioned, no good historian of Early Modern Europe would accept the notion of a rising middle class in the early sixteenth century. Second, no one, historian or otherwise, should accept Paris's assertion of the nature of this mythical group's mentality. Unlike his model (Lucien Goldmann), Paris provides no contemporary documentation to support his claims for the group's "social schizophrenia." (Citing Lefebvre—himself a very biased and, in this case, uninformed "historian"—is obviously not sufficient.) Third, Mauss's analysis of potlatch has been questioned, and largely rejected, by modern anthropologists.[17] Hence, among other things, Bataille's/Paris's argument that an urge toward unrecuperable expenditure is necessarily "primitive"—much less, as Paris would imply, "popular" or peasantlike—becomes extremely dubious. One has only to recall the lavish, conspicuous consumption of goods practiced by many medieval and even Renaissance nobles to realize that such treatment of property was not limited to the people before or even during the Renaissance. Indeed, one might come closer to a historically correct understanding of this passage in Rabelais's text if one proposed to see in the conflicting views of Panurge and Pantagruel representations of the conflicting economic mentalities of the medieval and even Renaissance nobility and people versus the sixteenth-century mercantile class.

Finally—and perhaps most important from the point of view of students of literature—the application of Bataille to chapter 2 (and of Marx to chapters 3–4) in order to make a non- (or pre- or anti-) capitalist of Panurge ignores entirely some of his other remarks later in the same text. In chapter 6, Pantagruel explains one of the laws of Moses, by which recently married men are excused from military service: "According to my judgment . . . the law was that for the first year [the newly married men] should enjoy all the pleasures to the full, have time to produce progeny [vacassent à production de lignage], and provide themselves with heirs [et feissent provision de heritiers]. Then, even if in the second year they were killed in the war, their name and coat of arms would be perpetuated by their children" (304; TL 59). "Production de lignage" and "provision de heritiers" certainly suggest a very "capitalistic" view of the function of marriage and legitimate offspring. Yet Panurge sounds every bit as capitalistic on the same subject just a few pages later. Having vowed that he will be "a great householder," "the perfect householder" ([un] grand mesnaiger, [le] mesnaiger parfaict) ·(306; TL 67), after having just shortly before laughed at the cry of "Thrift! Thrift!" (mesnaige, mesnaige!) (293; TL 30), he subsequently announces that he wants to get married because (in part) "there's no other way of getting legitimate sons and daughters, by whom I can hope to perpetuate my name and armorial bearings, and to whom I can leave my inheritances and acquisitions—and I shall get some fine ones too, one of these days, without a doubt" (312; *TL* 79). Indeed, such an understanding of the function of children closely resembles the very "capitalistic" remarks of Gargantua near the end of the novel, when the King of Utopie speaks of parents who raised their daughters carefully, "hoping in due course to marry them to the sons of their neighbours and old friends. . . . They had looked forward to the birth of children from these happy marriages, who would inherit and preserve not only the morals of their fathers and mothers, but also their goods and lands" (419; *TL* 321–22).

As this passage shows, Panurge's economic ideology in the *Third Book* can be every bit as "capitalistic" as Pantagruel's (and Gargantua's). To look at him as the expression of a peasant economic stance (and to look at his "economic ideology" in chapter 2 as "popular") is simply to concentrate on part of the text to the exclusion of the rest (as well as to ignore the findings of modern historiography and anthropology).[18]

Indeed, at one point Panurge even seems to be the quintessential labor-exploiting capitalist: having spent 600,000 maravedis on an earring, "he fed [this expenditure], like any tyrant or lawyer, on the sweat and blood of his subjects" (305; *TL* 63). In defending his destructive, uncontrolled expenditure of money in chapter 2 (or in praising lending and borrowing in order to cover for his own indebtedness in chapters 3 and 4), Panurge is clearly being "disorderly," refusing to submit to the "order" that Pantagruel has established everywhere else in Dipsodie. Yet to explain (some of) his economic positions as an expression of "the people" (or at least a nostalgia for their way of life) is, at best, a misuse of Rabelais's text.[19]

Reste seulement le *Quart Livre* à traiter.

Unlike the gap of over a decade that separated the *Third Book* (1546) from *Gargantua* (1535), the *Fourth Book* (1552) followed the *Third* by only a half-dozen years. It demonstrates a somewhat greater use of popular culture than its immediate predecessor, yet is still far from returning to the style of *Pantagruel* or the first part of *Gargantua*. It is the only one of the four narratives to have a formal dedication—to Odet de Coligny, cardinal of

Chastillon, member of a powerful family who eventually became one of the major figures among the French Protestants.
Perhaps Rabelais felt that Coligny was somewhat more open to
popular culture, though it shouldn't be imagined that he wrote
the *Fourth Book* specifically for the cardinal. It is more likely
that, having had a chance to judge his public's response to his
and others' works, Rabelais concluded that at least limited use of
popular culture in his fourth narrative would not jeopardize its
chances of being taken seriously by his intended readers.

Be that as it may, the *Fourth Book*, like the *Third*, still demonstrates a great familiarity with antiquity. Names are not dropped
with quite the frequency and abundance that distinguished the
1546 work, but they still appear far more often than in the first
two narratives. Disease is still excluded—in the Prologue, the
narrator addresses himself simply to "good people" (439; *QL*
11)[20]—and juxtaposition of disease with "the important" is
soundly condemned. When speaking with the Papimanes, Friar
John tells a story about several beggars he knew at Seuillé. Returning from their day's begging, one "fat rascal got up and proclaimed [to his fellow beggars] that he had made three whole
shillings. 'Oh yes,' replied his companions, 'but you've got God's
lucky leg.'—As if there were some divine and fortunate power
concealed in a leg that was all ulcerated and decayed." Pantagruel
reacts immediately, and strongly: "When you are going to tell us
stories like that . . . please remember to bring a basin. That one
nearly made me sick. Fancy using the name of God in such a
filthy, abominable context! Ugh, I say ugh! If such misuse of
words is the habit in your monkery, please leave it there, and
don't bring it with you out of the cloister" (555; *QL* 207).

Evocations of a popular-culture Land of Cockaigne, like the
world in Pantagruel's mouth, where food is in abundance and
men are freed from the constant need to work, also continue to
be absent from Rabelais's narrative world as of the *Fourth Book*.
The absence is perhaps even more obvious here than in the preceding narrative, however, in that several of the lands depicted in
Les Navigations de Panurge, a work from which Rabelais drew
material for the *Fourth* (and what was published as the *Fifth*)
Book, are in fact based upon this popular culture image; there
are islands where the rivers flow with milk and wine, cakes and

cheeses grow on the trees, and so forth. In other words, even here, where it would have been easy for Rabelais to include an important element of popular culture in his work, since the models were already present to him (and his readers), he chose not to do so.[21]

Also absent from the *Fourth Book*, as from its two predecessors, is any serious criticism or humiliation of figures of power and authority. Bakhtin makes much of the tale about François Villon and Friar Tappecoue (B 263–70), in which Villon tricks Tappecoue and eventually causes his death because Tappecoue refused to lend him a costume for the passion play Villon was staging. Bakhtin does not bother to point out several important details, however. First, Friar Tappecoue is only a sacristan (478; *QL* 82), a very lowly figure in the church hierarchy, and therefore hardly a figure of power and authority (such as the popes who figure among those humiliated in Epistemon's Hell). Second, this François Villon is presented as someone who works with "the powers that be": if he goes around requesting clothing to serve as costumes for his players, it is only after he has cleared everything with the local mayor and aldermen and has received express permission to do so (ibid.). Finally, and as even Bakhtin notes (though he fails to pursue its implications), the story of Villon's revenge on Tappecoue is told by *Lord* Basché, who recounts it to his domestics in order to encourage them to help him drive away the men sent by the "fat prior of St. Louant" to summon him to court (476; *QL* 79). Though Bakhtin speaks of the "utopian kingdom of absolute equality and freedom" (B 264), the fact of Rabelais's text is that Lord Basché invokes the legend of François Villon in order to obtain help in maintaining his power and authority (against the prior's attempt to deprive him of it). Furthermore, just as he describes to his domestics the beating of a humble sacristan, rather than an important prelate, so he is encouraging them to brutalize the "bum-baliffs" sent by the prior, rather than the prior himself. For that matter, Basché begins his tale about Villon by noting that "in his old age Master Francis Villon retired to Saint-Maixent in Poitou, *under the protection of a worthy churchman who was abbot of that place*" (478; *QL* 82; my italics). If the entire passage is examined, it becomes clear that Basché (and Rabelais) are not using Tappecoue to "in-

carnate the spirit of the Gothic age" (B 268), the "serious" hierarchy of the Catholic church, or any other aspect of the establishment. Tappecoue incarnates nothing but what he is, an
ornery, lowly sacristan.

Mention of sex in the *Fourth Book* is as limited as in the *Third*.
When Dindenault succeeds in thoroughly angering Panurge, the
latter asks the merchant what he would do if he found Panurge
making love to his wife (461; *QL* 52); Panurge's descriptive and
precise language leaves no doubt about exactly what would be
taking place. When Homenaz, the chief of the Papimanes, gives
Pantagruel some of their special pears to take back to Utopie,
Friar John observes: "I should be just as pleased . . . if he would
give us two or three cartloads of his girls." Homenaz asks what
he would do with them, and the monk replies: "We would bleed
them half-way between their big-toes with certain prodding
tools that work wonders. . . . In that way we'd graft some Good-
Christian children on them, and the race in our land would mul-
tiply" (565–66; *QL* 223). Again, the sex is all talk, and the talk
comes only from characters outside the locus of power and
authority.

There is something of a loosening up on this point in the case
of the narrator, however. He dares more than an occasional
sexual double-entendre in his description of the relationships
between the inhabitants of Ennasin Island (chap. 9), and recounts Priapus's very erotic equivocations on the word "hatchet"
(444–46; *QL* 23–25). Important characters are even described
as reacting favorably to the garden god's erotic anecdotes: "At
these words all the venerable gods and goddesses burst out
laughing, like a microcosm of flies, and Vulcan with his twisted
leg performed three or four pretty little jigs on the daïs, for the
love of his mistress" (446; *QL* 25).[22] The narrator also recounts
the story of Frederick Barbarossa's humiliation of the Milanese
(544; *QL* 189; the donkey and the fig leaf), which is about as
"erotically obscene" as Panurge's remarks concerning what he
would do with Dindenault's wife. At one point, the narrator even
seems to bring back the "good old days" of popular culture's
respectability in *Pantagruel*. His story of the young devil, the
farmer, and his wily peasant wife (545–49; *QL* 190–96) very
much recalls the tale of the lion, the fox, and the old woman in

the first novel. Still, such inclusions of sex are relatively infrequent, and mention of it never involves Pantagruel and those in power.[23]

The aspect of popular culture that makes the greatest comeback in the *Fourth Book* is excrement. As with sex, the characters in the narrative who talk about feces all operate outside the locus of power and authority. When Homenaz asks his visitors to admire the Papimanes' prized Decretales, Panurge and Friar John tell stories in which pages of the work are used as toilet paper (558–59; *QL* 212). (The other characters, though they also mock the Decretales, do not mention feces in doing so.) Panurge recounts a story—and recites his *dizain*—about Janin de Quinquenays' "pissing on his wife Quelot's backside" (542; *QL* 185–86). Dindenault includes the excrement of his sheep when detailing the usefulness of their every part (464; *QL* 58), just as Xenomanes includes Quaresmeprenant's feces in his anatomization of the monster (chaps. 30–31). Even Epistemon, normally a somewhat more restrained and dignified character, announces "quite clearly," as Homenaz goes on *ad nauseam* in praise of the Decretales: "For want of a close stool I'm forced to retire. This stuffing has relaxed my bumgut. I shan't be long" (558; *QL* 211).

Epistemon's remark—as well as Panurge and Friar John's mention of feces in association with the Decretales and the monk's remark concerning what he would like to do with some of Homenaz's serving girls—are all made at one of the banquets included in the *Fourth Book*, that organized by Homenaz to celebrate the arrival of the *Thalamege* and its crew. Though, as noted, there is more "free and jocular speech" at this banquet than at the one held for Hippothadée, Rondibilis, and Trouillogan in the *Third Book*, the fact remains that there is no "democratic spirit" here, no breaking down of "the limits between man and man." Pantagruel's crew have all taken a dislike to Homenaz, and if they refer to sex and excrement it is not because they have come together in one spirit of freedom and brotherhood, but rather, because they are trying very hard to irritate their host—and succeeding quite well.

There are other group dining scenes in the *Fourth Book*, but again, they are all far removed from the popular culture banquet. Generally they are brief instances at which conversation (the very essence of the popular culture banquet), if held, is not reported. This is true of the meals provided: by the Thalasiens for the departing members of Pantagruel's expedition (452; *QL* 35–36); by Pantagruel for Malicorne and his men (457–59; *QL* 46–49); at the cabaret on Ennasin Island, where a wedding is being celebrated (470–71; *QL* 69–70); by the Macreons for Pantagruel and his crew (504–5; *QL* 127); by Pantagruel for his men after he has killed the giant "spouter" and they have landed on Savage Island (525; *QL* 159). Bakhtin tries to tie the episode of Lord Basché into the carnival, banquet aspects of popular culture, but the fact remains, as already pointed out, that Basché does not allow a carnival banquet, a "utopian," "democratic" spirit of freedom, but rather, makes use of this tradition to achieve his own very nonpopular, upper-class, hierarchy-maintaining ends.

Again, the narrator is also somewhat freer with his mention of matters excremental. Recounting Bringuenarilles's last days, he remarks: "He had digested the kettles and saucepans well enough, as was evident from the bubbles and sediment in the four barrels of urine that he had filled that morning on two occasions" (488; *QL* 98).[24] He repeats the report of Queen Niphleseth's spies that Quaresmeprenant "had made a landing [on Savage Island] and was amusing himself by inspecting the spouters' [*physetères*'] urine" (539; *QL* 181). On the Island of Ruach, he relates, "they do not shit, piss or spit. . . . But, on the other hand, they poop, fart, and belch most copiously" (541; *QL* 184). The narrator also tells how Messer Gaster "referred [those who worship him as a god] to his close-stool, to see, to examine and philosophically to consider what kind of god they could discover in his faeces" (579; *QL* 245). Excrement is more freely mentioned in the *Fourth Book* than in the *Third*, but as in *Gargantua* after chapter 12, and unlike in *Pantagruel*, it is never brought in contact with Pantagruel or the locus of authority. In certain episodes of the fourth narrative, moreover, episodes involving Panurge, it seems to take on particularly negative connotations.

Panurge undergoes a general downgrading and exclusion of his own from *Pantagruel* to the *Fourth Book*. In Rabelais's first narrative, as already mentioned, Panurge becomes the dominant figure. It is he who directs much of the war against the Dipsodes, he to whom even Pantagruel turns for help. In the *Third Book*, Panurge operates more or less on a par with Pantagruel. He shows respect for his master (e.g., 302; *TL* 56), and Pantagruel certainly never asks him for assistance, but the two engage more or less as equals in the discussions concerning Panurge's possible future marriage.

This parity altogether vanishes by the *Fourth Book*. During the great tempest, Pantagruel holds onto the *Thalamege*'s rudder and guides the ship through the storm; Panurge, terrified, sits on the deck and blubbers, doing nothing to aid the crew. When a giant "spouter" (*physetère*) swims toward the *Thalamege*, Pantagruel dispatches it with several well-aimed harpoons; Panurge again blubbers in fear, crying, "We're all done for" (521; *QL* 153). When the ship encounters the frozen words (chap. 55), Pantagruel is intrigued and wants to sail closer to understand the mystery; Panurge, again, can only utter variations on "We are lost" (567; *QL* 225). As a result of his uncontrolled fear in the face of danger, Panurge fails to assist his companions in their efforts to defend their microsociety. In a narrative that places so much emphasis upon participating in the general defense of society against outside attack, and that provides so many opportunities for such participation, Panurge, by his repeated failure to join these efforts, is certainly presented as being inferior to Pantagruel, or even Friar John.[25]

Excrement is closely linked with the fear that keeps Panurge from participating in the defense of his small society. During the tempest, as he sits on the deck and blubbers, Panurge finally becomes so terrified that he beshits himself (493; *QL* 107). At the end of the novel, Friar John has the crew set off a volley of cannon; Panurge, down in the hold, is so frightened by the explosion that he again loses control of his sphincter muscles (594; *QL* 267). As a result, excrement takes on a doubly negative connotation in the *Fourth Book*. On the one hand, it is associated with a downgraded character (Panurge); on the other, it is related to a fear that keeps one from working for the defense of one's society. The narrator reinforces these negative connotations with his anecdotes about Pantolfe de la Cassine and Edward V (594–96; *QL* 267–69). In each case, excrement is presented as the result of fear.

The association of Messer Gaster (and his worshipers) with

excrement introduces another point concerning popular culture that is new in *Gargantua and Pantagruel* as of the *Fourth Book*. Throughout Rabelais's fourth narrative one finds examples of individuals who are devoted to the physical to the exclusion of "higher things." First there is Epistemon's anecdote about Friar Lardon, who sees nothing of interest in the artistic and architectural splendors of Renaissance Florence, but can only talk about the food and female flesh of his native Amiens (473–74; *QL* 73–75). Later the crew of the *Thalamege* encounter the Andouilles, who worship a flying pig that shouts "Mardigras!" and throws pots of mustard (538; *QL* 180); the citizens of Ruach, for whom a good sack of wind—their nourishment—is "like a Holy Grail" (542; *QL* 185); and, of course, Gaster, a stomach worshipped by the Engastrimythes and the Gastrolatres. Especially in these last three instances it is made quite clear that the individuals involved do not concern themselves with the metaphysical, but only with the physical, and quite specifically, with the satisfaction of their own most basic physical needs (nourishment). Pantagruel compares the Gastrolatres on this point to Polyphemus, "into whose mouth Euripides put these words: I only sacrifice to myself—to the gods never—and to this belly of mine, the greatest of all the gods" (574; *QL* 237). Though the comparison is directed only at the Gastrolatres, it is applicable to all the peoples mentioned above: they are all concerned with the satisfaction of their physical needs to the exclusion of any concern about what or who is outside or around them.[26] In this sense, they are all made to look even more self-centered and indifferent to their fellow man by their implicit contrast with the society encountered earlier on Ennasin Island (chap. 9). At that stop, each individual was defined by his or her relationship to some other inhabitant, and the result, their governor explains, is that "from this country, in case of need, more than three hundred thousand could march, all related to one another, and all of one family" (468; *QL* 65).

I have tried to develop at length the implications of this aspect of the *Fourth Book* elsewhere, but the change from the previous narratives along these lines can be summarized here briefly as follows. As of *Gargantua*, Rabelais demonstrates a considerable preoccupation with social order and cohesion and its threatened dissolution. Picrochole is repeatedly condemned for having sundered the "alliances" that previously bound Utopie and Lerné together—and that kept other powers in line out of respect for this alliance. When Grandgousier and Ulrich Gallet talk about the disruption of social order that Picrochole brings about with his invasion of Utopie, they repeatedly assert that God must have abandoned Picrochole, such that Satan could take control of him and, through him, attempt to disrupt social cohesion.

In the *Third Book* this preoccupation with social order and the forces that threaten it continues, but now the disruptive agent is Panurge, who tries to escape his military duty by getting married and so, as Pantagruel points out, refuses to consider his duty to his fellow men, to work with them for the protection of society as a whole. Again, Panurge's antisocietal, self-centered attitude is attributed, by Pantagruel, to the workings of Satan.

Finally, in the *Fourth Book*, Rabelais presents a whole series of social "pairs"—Bringuenarilles/Ruach, the Papefigues/the Papimanes, the Andouilles/Quaresmeprenant, and several others —each of which is breaking assunder, in part, at least, because these various peoples have turned in completely upon themselves, evincing no concern whatsoever for anything or anyone else. The implications of such an attitude are brought out by the microcosm on board the *Thalamege*. Like these various peoples, Panurge, during any crisis—the tempest, the attack of the giant *physetère*—loses all concern for anyone, or anything, other than himself and his own physical well-being. As a result, he does not work with the other crew members to defend the microcosmic society as a whole. Indeed, he cannot, for he falls victim to such fear that he can only sit and blubber. Several times the other crew members deplore the potential danger that such behavior poses to the entire ship's company.

With the continual comparisons of Panurge to animals— sheep, monkeys, etc.—Rabelais seems to be suggesting that God has abandoned Panurge, that he has withdrawn from him the Reason that distinguished men from animals (to the sixteenth-century mind) and that would have allowed Panurge, unlike sheep or monkeys, to get control of his "animal" emotions (like fear) to the extent of being able to function with and for his fellow men. Similarly, several of the materialistic peoples encountered by the crew of the *Thalamege* have abandoned God—or been abandoned by him—to worship instead the material (such as food) rather than the metaphysical. In a narrative that puts so much emphasis upon individuals working with each other to defend their society against external threats, the self-centered "bodily materialism" of these peoples must also appear in a negative light.

This should probably be kept in mind when considering the final banquet in the *Fourth Book*. The wind having died down as the ship passes Chaneph, the crew, with nothing to do, take to asking trivial, rhetorical questions ("How can a man make water when he has no urge to?") (585–86; *QL* 254–55). Pantagruel has a banquet set up, and his men, having devoured it, declare that all their questions have been answered. Pantagruel himself remarks: "Since you're contented with this easy solution of the questions proposed . . . so am I" (590–91; *QL* 261). There is no "banquet freedom" of language or action here, no "democratic," "utopian" spirit of equality. Even worse, however, with Pantagruel's description of his crew's reaction to the food as "this easy solution," it would seem that Rabelais had altogether lost faith in the popular culture banquet to the extent that it, like any decent banquet, must be involved with—indeed, celebrate— food, drink, and "bodily materialism."

In this respect, one might wonder whether Rabelais saw such self-centered materialism to be an aspect—and hence a negative quality—of popular culture. Certainly, some modern writers have described medieval and Renaissance popular culture as materialistic, as opposed to transcendental. Bakhtin is a primary example, of course, with his centering of popular culture around the "material bodily lower stratum." In this way, the Soviet critic was able to reinforce his opposition between "the people" and "the establishment" (with the latter's "repressive, ruling-class" religion). Even less biased historians have recognized a heavily materialistic quality in popular culture, however, among them Carlo Ginzburg (61) and Robert Muchambled (118). Whether or not Renaissance popular culture was indeed primarily materialistic and nontranscendental, Rabelais may well have seen it as such. Given his emphasis in the *Fourth Book* upon the importance of working with one's fellow man for the defense of society as a whole, as well as his presentation of "bodily materialism" as that which draws one away from participating in such cooperative efforts, as that which indicates that God has abandoned his efforts to join men together as mutually sustaining members of society, it is possible that, with the *Fourth Book*, Rabelais had developed yet another reason to distrust and devalue popular culture.

PART III

Bakhtin's *Rabelais* in the Light of Soviet History; *Pantagruel* in the Light of Bakhtin's *Dostoevsky*

Whatever its merits, Bakhtin's *Rabelais* is seriously flawed by two major weaknesses. First, the work's basic theoretical construct proves to be without foundation in the social history from which Bakhtin claimed to derive it. Second, by not acknowledging the very marked shift in attitude toward popular culture from *Pantagruel* to the subsequent narratives, Bakhtin allowed his interpretation of Rabelais's work to become ever more distant from the text of that work itself.

The reader familiar with the rapidly growing esteem accorded Bakhtin by much of the modern critical establishment might well ask how so respected and admired a scholar could have overlooked so much. Though Bakhtin presents his interpretation of Rabelais as founded upon an understanding of sixteenth-century popular culture (and society in general), he offers little in the way of contemporary documentation or evidence to support his description and interpretation of that culture.[1] The relative frequency with which he cites each of the four Rabelaisian novels suggests in itself that there must be some significant change in the use of popular culture from the first to the later narratives. Could Bakhtin really have been so unobservant a critic as not to have seen what his own citing of Rabelais's texts suggests?

I don't believe so. Not at all. And if I have spent much time in the preceding pages demonstrating why Bakhtin's *Rabelais* is not an example of good historical criticism, I would now like to come to the book's defense. *Rabelais and His World* is a good book, but it remains to be shown what kind of good book, what kind of book, it really is.

Or it did remain to be shown until the appearance in late 1984 of Katerina Clark and Michael Holquist's analytical biography, *Mikhail Bakhtin*. In their chapter on *Rabelais and His World* (CH 295–320), they situate Bakhtin's presentation of Rabelais in the context of the political and intellectual climate of the Soviet Union at the time of the book's composition. Their presentation may be summarized as follows.

In the early 1930s, Stalin's government established "socialist realism" as the new aesthetic for the Soviet artist. All art, especially literature and especially the novel, was henceforth to be "party-minded" (CH 270). Furthermore, literature was to draw on folklore for some of its models, since folklore contains "the unwritten compositions of the toiling man" (CH 272). For the Soviet government, these "folk" were of a very particular sort. The folk hero's function was "to affirm the status quo and impress the public with his monumentalness" (ibid.). Therefore the official Soviet view of the folk and their culture was characterized by stability, homogeneity of purpose, and the like, all "virtues" that the government sought to instill in its citizens.

While the "folk" began to figure as an important element in socialist realism, and Soviet iconography in general (CH 310), certain aspects of folk culture most certainly did not. "In 1932–34, when the guidelines for socialist realism were being formulated, official spokesmen cautioned writers against the literary practice of showing sex and the bodily functions, which was euphemistically called 'naturalism' or 'zoologism.' In consequence, explicit sex relations were virtually taboo in Stalinist novels." Stalinist society was marked by an ever-increasing puritanism and idealization, an "emphasis on transcending the physical body" (CH 312).

It was also marked by a preoccupation with social "purification." By 1936–38, Stalin's purges of "undesirable" elements among the inhabitants of the Soviet Union, his attempts to create a culturally, ethnically, and intellectually homogeneous society had reached heights that even his ally across the Oder might have admired.

This is the historical context of *Rabelais and His World*. By the mid-1930s, Stalin's government had managed to arrive at a position diametrically opposed in almost every way to the ideals of the Revolution. Yet it also managed to provide, or at least indicate to Bakhtin, the very material for a critique of its position. "In 1934 Gorky had cited *Gargantua* and *Pantagruel* as examples of the influence of 'oral folk literature' on written literature, an influence that he wanted to see more of in socialist realism. Moreover, he found exemplified in *Gargantua* and *Pantagruel* the sort of folk tradition where the lower orders 'have acquired the courage to ridicule their masters.'" From there on in, Bakhtin had only to follow the lead so "officially" proffered, albeit to his own very different goals. As Clark and Holquist remark with regard to *Rabelais and His World*, Bakhtin "coopts the ideas and rhetoric of his age and uses them to his own ends" (CH 313).

If the folk were held up for praise in Soviet literature and iconography in general, Bakhtin would turn his attention to popular culture in works of literature that had been lauded specifically, and officially, for their inclusion of the folk. Yet the people and their culture, as Bakhtin presented them, bore no resemblance whatsoever to the "folk" as officially depicted. Bakhtin's people and their culture, in the sixteenth century and all times, are distinguished by ambivalence, the ability to contain at one time even the strongest oppositions and contradictions. They are characterized by instability and change, a dynamism that moves ever forward to the new. They are associated with a mockery of serious, single-minded dogma, pompous officialdom. In short, they are the incarnation of the spirit of permanent revolution. Some of Bakhtin's contemporaries had "welcomed the Revolution and sought some sort of permanent revolution in society or culture as well." "They looked . . . to the end of bourgeois society with its hypocritical morality, its conventionality, its fuddy-duddy cultural and intellectual establishment, its love of material comfort, and its complacency." "Their concept of revolution was a dramatic thrust for perpetual renewal, for confounding canons, for randomness and diversity" (CH 316). If the Stalinist government could create a mythological "folk" who incarnated all the qualities that it sought to instill in the Soviet citizenry, so Bakhtin could create his own mythology of a people who exemplified all the principles of revolution. As Clark and Holquist have noted, "While opposing one idealized conception of the folk, Bakhtin's own counter-image is no less idealized." If Stalin's ideologists moved to an ever greater puritanism and denial of the human body, Bakhtin's image of the officially glorified people would be "dripping with urine and feces" (CH 310). If Stalin worked toward a "purification" of Soviet culture and society, Bakhtin's popular culture would be open, able and willing to include and contain contradictions, a joyful exaltation of heterogeneity.

At the very beginning of their book, Clark and Holquist had stated that "ostensibly, most of [Bakhtin's] writings are acts of scholarly erudition and exercises in literary or linguistic theory, but underneath they are personal manifestos, often with a political or philosophical message" (CH 2). More specifically of *Rabelais and His World* they remark that "it cannot fail to be in part a comment on its times." "It represents Bakhtin's most comprehensive critique to date of Stalinist culture" (CH 305). Indeed, as should by now be readily apparent, the "unchanging, serious, official medieval culture" of which Bakhtin speaks was clearly meant to suggest that of the Stalinist regime.

Yet, as Clark and Holquist add, "although there is undoubtedly an element of political allegory in *Rabelais*, the work cannot be written off as an anti-Bolshevik or anti-Stalinist tract. Nor can it be reduced to a mere commentary on Bakhtin's times" (CH 315). With his "reconstruction" of medieval and Renaissance popular culture, Bakhtin summarized the spirit and ideals of the "permanent revolutionists." By presenting this spirit and these ideals as the essence of medieval and Renaissance popular culture, he was able to introduce and even exalt them under the cover of the official glorification to which the "folk" had recently been subject.

"Insofar as a single topic can be defined as the subject of his thought," Clark and Holquist began their study, "[Bakhtin] was a philosopher of freedom" (CH 11). With regard to *Rabelais and His World*, they can, understandably, continue: "Thus, in a time of increasing regimentation, Bakhtin wrote of freedom. . . . At a time when literature was composed of mandated canons, he wrote of smashing all norms and canons and ridiculed the pundits who upheld them. At a time when everyone was told to look 'higher' and to deny the body and its dictates, he extolled the virtues of the everyday and advocated reveling in the basic functions of what he called the 'lower bodily stratum'" (CH 312).

I began this discussion of its historical context by affirming that, in my opinion, *Rabelais and His World* is a good book. I do very seriously believe that. As I have tried to show, relying on the study of Professors Clark and Holquist, *Rabelais and His World* is an allegorical work of political criticism and theory. To the extent that the allegory is transparent, Bakhtin's writing and presentation of this work was a highly courageous act. Indeed, if I may paraphrase one of his own remarks about *Gargantua and Pantagruel*, his dissertation—or at least the writing of it—is among the most fearless in the history of literary scholarship. I cannot accord the work any real value as historical criticism (or at least as an interpretation of Rabelais; it has suggested approaches that led to more valid analyses of other works). Nonetheless, as a critique of Stalinist policy, it remains a fascinating and admirable creation. Many respectable works of literary criticism amount to far less.

The above explanation of Bakhtin's interpretation of *Gargantua and Pantagruel* may provoke one question. "Even given that Bakhtin had extraliterary critical reasons for presenting the interpretation of Rabelais that he offered," one might begin, "is there really no basis in the text itself for his analysis? Is it simple chance that has caused various critics to find in Rabelais's works a spirit of revolution?" Bakhtin (and Beaujour) have claimed that his texts express the revolt of the people against the oppression of the establishment. Lefebvre (and Paris) have seen in those texts the revolt of a middle class against their social and political superiors. Abel Lefranc hailed Rabelais as the spokesman for rational atheism against the suppressive regime of universal (in Europe) Christianity. Various modern critics cite Rabelais as an exponent of new theories of language and literature, as well as a debunker of the previous theories. Is it just happenstance, even given that the particular spirit they claim to find often varies, that so many readers of Rabelais have attributed to his works a revolutionary fermentation?

This is the point where I might indulge my fascination with Stanley Fish's "Interpreting the *Variorum*" and simply refer readers to that provocative essay.[2] In it, Professor Fish advances the radical hypothesis that, in fact, literary (or any other) texts *do not* in and of themselves contain meaning. Rather, he asserts, texts are collections of signs. Each reader brings to each text a set of interpretive codes, according to which these signs appear to mean one or several things. But the signs in themselves, and hence the text, do not possess any one or several inherent, "natural" meanings. Viewed from this perspective, it could be argued that there is indeed no revolutionary spirit in *Gargantua and Pantagruel* (or anything else, for that matter). If various critics have claimed to find such a spirit in those texts, it is because that was the nature of the interpretive codes with which they came equipped as they approached the text.

My summary does not begin to do justice to Professor Fish's argument. Yet, if I might be so unfair as to dispute his stance through my own resumé of it, I believe that there are certain things that are actually, really "in" certain texts, such that these texts will always have the same effect on all (astute) readers. One of the things that I believe to be actually, really in *Pantagruel* is an ideological pluralism that can easily lend itself to an anti-establishment interpretation of the text. Whether or not I am able to prove this hypothesis remains to be seen.

If Bakhtin had not had ulterior, nonliterary critical motives for writing the Rabelais book as he did, motives that may have taken precedence with him over the presentation of "interpretive truth," I believe that, given the work he had already done (primarily on Dostoevsky), he could have provided some valuable observations on Rabelais's narratives. (One might argue that "dealing with literature strictly as literature," "extracting strictly literary truth," would never have been an interest or even a possibility for Bakhtin, given his very nature. For the purposes of this discussion such arguments are really beside the point.) Though I'm sure I will provoke yet further scoffs from fervent Bakhtinians by doing so, I would like to conclude this study with a "Bakhtinian" analysis of *Gargantua and Pantagruel*. I do not pretend to offer something that Bakhtin himself might have written. I would, however, like to present this analysis in very sincere homage to him.

Unquestionably one of the most interesting aspects of Bakhtin's *Dostoevsky* (1929; revised 1963) is the notion of "polyphony," or "dialogism." According to Bakhtin, Dostoevsky's novels are distinguished by the simultaneous, unresolved presence of mutually independent—and sometimes even conflicting—points of view. "A plurality of independent and unmerged voices and consciousnesses, a genuine polyphony of fully valid voices is in fact the chief characteristic of Dostoevsky's novels" (*Dos* 6). Many authors have produced works in which different characters express different points of view, of course. Dostoevsky's uniqueness, Bakhtin argues, is that whereas other writers always cause one point of view to predominate, to be indicated as the "right" stance, beside which all the others are dismissed or subordinated, Dostoevsky allows the various different voices to exist together in his narrative world with the full strength of their respective individualities (though he may well indicate a preference for one over the rest). To use Bakhtin's own terms, Dostoevsky allows "dialogism" of ideas throughout his works, rather than imposing upon them "monologism," the reign of a single, privileged point of view ("voice").

In his *Problems of Dostoevsky's Poetics*, Bakhtin imitates the methodology that he attributes to Dostoevsky. He brings out a variety of different voices that he finds to be playing off each other in various of the works. Like Dostoevsky as he describes him, Bakhtin does not attempt to privilege any one voice or voices over the others, either by claiming that they represent the thought of the author himself or by applying some other scale of values. Having praised Dostoevsky for his ability—and willingness—to let different, even conflicting voices express themselves in unresolved opposition through his writings, Bakhtin does his best to bring out these voices without any resolving or subordinating of his own.

In this sense his *Rabelais* is very different. Rather than seeking to demonstrate the presence of a plurality of voices in *Gargantua and Pantagruel*, Bakhtin concerns himself with asserting the existence of only two: "official" culture and "popular" culture. Never does he allow for the possibility that Rabelais, like Dostoevsky, might be permitting these two points of view to exist in a state of "dialogism," to function wholly and independently without authorial privileging or subordination. Unlike his treatment of Dostoevsky's novels, Bakhtin promptly reduces the narrative world of *Gargantua and Pantagruel* to monologism. If both "official" and "popular" culture are present in these works, he argues, Rabelais very clearly and unambiguously always sides with the latter and against the former and always means his reader to do the same.

As I have tried to show, this is in fact not the case. In *Pantagruel* there is a real "dialogism" on the point of learned and popular culture, both being allowed to function independently and without hierarchization even though they are sometimes in real opposition. As of the midpoint in *Gargantua*, Rabelais's narratives do succumb to "monologism," but not at all that ascribed to them by Bakhtin; henceforth, though popular culture may continue to be present, it is always kept in check and downgraded by a very nonambivalent, "monologic," establishment point of view.

To conceive of *Pantagruel's* pluralism strictly in terms of the learned-popular dichotomy is to do injustice to that work's richness, however. (Bakhtin did not settle for bringing out simply one set of voices in Dostoevsky's novels.) I would like to conclude this study with an effort to demonstrate *Pantagruel's* real polyphony (and not just diaphony).

First, though, and although I do not wish to be seen as nit-picking, I would like to set aside Bakhtin's term "polyphony." I do not know how much he knew about counterpoint—he is quick to stress that he uses "polyphonic" only as a metaphor (*Dos* 22)—but the presence of simultaneous independent and even contradictory voices really is somewhat different from the actual nature of musical counterpoint.

In tonal counterpoint (the most universally admired practitioner of which was certainly J. S. Bach) one does not really have several different "fully valid" musical lines. There is usually only one fully developed melody; the other voices, though distinct, are of subordinate melodic interest and are more a function of the harmonic needs of the principle melody than independent melodic developments.

Bakhtin's "polyphony" more closely resembles modal counterpoint (developed to its heights by such figures as Palestrina, Byrd, and Tallis). Here, indeed, one encounters multiple different, "fully valid" musical lines operating simultaneously; the melodic development of most of the lines is not subordinated to the harmonic needs of a principle voice. Most of the voices do function and develop in a state of equality.

Even so, however, these voices can never be independent, an important criterion in Bakhtin's definition of his polyphony. Though one line is usually not subordinated to another, all must function within the restrictions of the rules of modal harmony: at any one point, no voice can wander off as it "chooses," totally independent of the part it must play in constituting the consonance of the moment.

In other words, Bakhtin's polyphony is much less restrictive than even modal counterpoint. Whereas the different voices in a Palestrina mass must fit into a greater consonance, or unified whole, the different points of view contained within a given Dostoevsky text may well not, according to Bakhtin, be resolvable as parts of one greater, unified whole.

Given the analysis presented in Part II, Section 1, above, popular and learned culture would actually appear to function in *Pantagruel* like model polyphony. They each have their own independent, internal logic and "validity," yet, because of the upper classes' "bi-culturalism" in the early sixteenth century, they can be understood together, even with their contradictions and conflicts, as belonging to one greater, unified (for the moment) whole (the upper-class bi-cultural consciousness).

Not all the pluralism in *Pantagruel* operates like modal counterpoint, however. Sometimes, as in Bakhtin's analysis of Dostoevsky, the simultaneous and conflicting voices cannot be understood as parts of one greater, coherent whole. For this reason I would prefer to speak of "pluralism" rather than "polyphony." I will try to illustrate its nature and presence in *Pantagruel* with the help of Thomas More's *Utopia*.

In her 1967 essay, "Bakhtine, le mot, le dialogue, et le roman," Julia Kristeva did much to introduce Bakhtin, and in particular his *Rabelais* and *Dostoevsky*, to the West.[3] One aspect of dialogism that she particularly emphasized is the inclusion in one text of voices that evoke and thereby draw in other, distinct texts. Bakhtin himself does not do much with this idea in his *Dostoevsky*, and he seems to forget about it almost altogether in his *Rabelais*. I believe this was an unfortunate oversight, however, for there is definite intertextuality in Rabelais's first narrative.

One work of literature that figures prominently in *Pantagruel* without ever being mentioned as such is Sir Thomas More's *Utopia* (1516). The country of which Gargantua is king, where

Pantagruel grows up, is given the name "Utopie," and the word is inserted in the text, often prominently, six times (174, 196, 201, 245, 262, 272; *P* 17, 48, 53, 126, 154, 169). In addition, one of the groups of people in Utopie is three times given the name "Amaurotes" (174, 247, 270; *P* 16, 130, 166), a place name borrowed from *Utopia*; Rabelais borrows the name "Achorie" (247; *P* 130) for the same purpose. It is highly likely that many of Rabelais's readers would already have been familiar with More's text. It would therefore seem safe to say that almost anyone likely to have read *Pantagruel* in 1532 would have noticed the allusions to More's work. Thus, one might ask why Rabelais chose to draw *Utopia* into his narrative world. Certainly, in part, he meant to pay tribute to one of the era's great humanists, but much more would seem to be involved. A brief recall of certain aspects of More's text is in order.

Perhaps the best-known element of More's treatise on the ideal government and state is his condemnation and exclusion of the institution of private ownership of goods and property. In Utopia, instead, all goods and means of production are held communally by the state. Able-bodied citizens must work on various projects necessary to the preservation of the state and its populace; in return, all inhabitants are provided for by the state.

More was convinced that as long as men were allowed the private ownership of property, there would be economic inequality; some men would have more than they needed for even a comfortable living, and others would have not even enough. To this state of things he attributed many of the ills of sixteenth-century society: if there was theft, it was because the poor were driven to steal to meet their needs; if there was social unrest, it was because beggars, with no stake in the welfare of society and plenty of time to make trouble, often fomented revolt; if there was moral corruption, it was because there were men—nobles, clerics, and others—who, not having to work, had both the time and the resources to indulge their every reprehensible whim. Communal control of property could remedy all these social ills. Since all men are provided for, no one has reason to steal; since all men are kept busy and have an interest in the continued health of the state, no man has the time or the incentive to stir up revolution or cultivate vice and immorality.

Yet equal distribution of property was not sufficient, in More's eyes, to prevent the corruption that he saw around him in sixteenth-century European society. Unlike in Voltaire's El Dorado, in Utopia there could be no luxury, even if everyone was able to enjoy it. The inhabitants of Utopia have only very simple plain clothes, all of which look largely the same. Nor is there any abundance of material possessions; each citizen receives a new outfit only once every two years. Similarly, the inhabitants are conditioned to hold gold in contempt; it is used to make chains for slaves. Thomas More clearly distrusted certain material pleasures in and of themselves, evidently convinced that the beauty of gold and fine clothing could of itself awaken a covetousness in the human spirit.

In relation to these aspects of *Utopia*, there is one further element of *Pantagruel* that needs to be mentioned. In the first of Rabelais's novels, money, goods, and personal property are the subject of little or no valuation or respect. In fact, when they do appear, it is usually only to be stolen, defaced, or destroyed. Shortly after his birth, the baby Pantagruel rips apart and eats one of his father's dairy cows (179; *P* 24), does the same to his father's pet bear (179–180; *P* 25), and, upon breaking out of his cradle, "broke that cradle of his into more than five hundred thousand pieces with a blow of his fist, which he struck at the middle of it in his rage, swearing that he would never go back into it" (181; *P* 26).

Still, the young Pantagruel's destructive treatment of personal property pales beside that of Panurge. From the first of his autobiographical tales, we see that Panurge is no respecter of other persons' property, or of goods or money in general. In order to escape from being roasted after having been captured by the Turks, he throws a brand from the fire into the lap of his sleeping turnspit. In addition to burning the Turk's genitals (much to Panurge's glee), the fire spreads until it threatens the entire house. Hearing of this catastrophe, the owner of the house hurries home, despairs at the prospect of losing all his belongings, and gives Panurge "six hundred seraphs . . . and some perfect diamonds and rubies" (216; *P* 79) to help him commit suicide. Panurge takes the gift, obliges the Turk, and then escapes from the house and the city. Meanwhile the fire spreads from the one house to some two thousand others. Describing all this later, Panurge recalls that he "saw the whole town burning, at which I was so glad that I almost shat myself for joy" (217; *P* 80).

Granted, such joy at the destruction of others' possessions is easily dismissed as the glee of revenge upon a captor (and of hatred for the infidel), but Panurge has no more respect for the possessions of those who have done him no injury (and are among his fellow Christians). Chapters 16 and 17 recount the various methods that Panurge employed to obtain money in Paris, "the commonest and most honest of which was by means of cunningly perpetrated larceny" (222; *P* 90). Indeed, he does not stop even at stealing from church poor boxes (226–27; *P* 96–98). In addition, he delights in ruining the fine clothes of wealthy Parisians (224, 225; *P* 92, 94–95). During his encounters with the "great Parisian lady" (chaps. 21–22), he steals the woman's rosary beads, "which were of lemonwood, with large gold beads at intervals of ten" (241; *P* 119) and later causes hundreds of dogs to urinate on her fine outfit.

Although Panurge enjoys stealing and destroying other persons' property, he has no interest in keeping it or other property for himself. At the point in his opening tale when he mentions that the owner of the burning house gave him 600 "seraphs," Epistemon interrupts with the question: "And where are they?" "'By St. John,' said Panurge, 'they are far enough off by now if they are still moving'" (216; *P* 79). After Panurge has explained to Alcofribas Nasier how he took far more coins from church poor boxes than he put in, the narrator asks: "And where the devil have they gone. . . . For you haven't half of one left" (227; *P* 98). Panurge replies that he has spent or given away all the money he stole plus that paid to him by the pope, some of it to provide dowries for old prostitutes, some to take Parisian ladies to court for wearing blouses that hid their breasts, and so on (228–29; *P* 98–101). If Panurge steals, it is not to acquire wealth for himself. He does not respect the property of others, but then, he does not really seem to have any interest in money, goods, and property himself.

Such an indifference toward material possessions could be explained in part by Rabelais's years as a member of the Franciscan order, distinguished by its vow of poverty and its rejection of worldly wealth.[4] If one recalls some of the passages from *Pantagruel* cited in Part II, Section 1, of this study, however—especially the comments of the cabbage farmer in the world inside Pantagruel's mouth and Epistemon's description of the inverted world of "his" hell, where "great lords" are not simply deprived of their wealth but humiliated, and that by the poor, who are given a moment of exultant triumph over them—it becomes easy to believe that the material wealth of the great lords was resented by those who did not have such wealth and the comforts and leisure it provided. If there seems to be real pleasure taken in stealing and destroying personal property in *Pantagruel*, it may, as much as anything, have been an expression of the sixteenth-century popular point of view. The poor would have seen personal property as part of the resented world of the "great lords" and therefore would have rejoiced at this property's destruction. In this sense, *Pantagruel* would reflect a mentality less concerned with changing the distribution of wealth (perhaps because such a redistribution was simply outside their realm of conception) than with depriving those who benefited from it of their envied and resented comfort, security, and leisure.

If this economic mentality, clearly arising from popular culture and directed against the upper classes, is accepted as present in *Pantagruel*, Rabelais's introduction of More's *Utopia* into the narrative world of his first novel comes off as far more than simply a homage to an admired scholar and statesman. More's sympathy with the economic plight of the poor, as well as his strong condemnation of the wealthy who did not work while the rest of mankind toiled from dawn to dusk,[5] would have made the drawing of his text into the world of *Pantagruel*, with its expressions of popular culture's complaints about the state of the poor and resentment of the state of the wealthy, particularly appropriate.

In other respects, however, More's Utopia is light-years removed from Rabelais's Utopie. Part of the reason for More's advocacy of communal ownership and equal distribution of wealth is that it will bring about the end of theft, of which he clearly disapproves; there is certainly no disapproval of Panurge's larceny, even when it is directed at the wealthy or the church. More condemns the nobility and others of the "leisure class" for not working and states that in Utopia all men must be kept busy; in Utopie, there is no glorification of labor, but rather a preoccupation with leisure and free time. In Utopia adolescents who become involved in prenuptial sex are disgraced before the entire community; no such stigma is attached to extramarital sexual activity in Utopie, whose very Prince indulges himself quite freely in such matters. More's Utopians have an almost absolute adversion to warfare. When threatened with attack, they either buy off the enemy with part of their large reserves of gold or else use this gold to hire mercenaries to do their warring for them. When the Dipsodes invade Utopia, Gargantua calls his son back from Paris to defend his homeland. No sooner does Pantagruel land than he and his companions begin a counteroffensive that involves them in much fighting and eventually includes an invasion of Dipsodie itself. The drawing of *Utopia* into *Pantagruel* seems very appropriate in certain respects; in others, it seems altogether contradictory.

Or pluralistic, if I might return to that term. Here, unlike the simultaneous presence of learned and popular culture, there is no greater, unified consciousness to which one can turn to make of *Pantagruel*'s pluralism a consonant polyphony. In Rabelais's first novel, on the points just enumerated, there is a definite "plurality of independent and unmerged voices and consciousnesses, a genuine polyphony [in Bakhtin's metaphoric sense] of fully valid voices."

This pluralism is different from the dialogism Bakhtin ascribes to Dostoevsky. Bakhtin feels that the Russian novelist actually expressed conflicting voices simultaneously, directly and openly; the Rabelais of *Pantagruel* only "allows" such pluralism by alluding to More's text and not specifically condemning those aspects of it which oppose voices already present in the text of *Pantagruel* itself. Still, in a text that often seems so "intertextual," drawing into its sphere of signification texts other than itself, there does seem to be a definite openness to—and more than just a tolerance of—opposition and contradiction, at least as regards Rabelais's use of *Utopia*. In short, there is in *Pantagruel* a real pluralism.

This pluralism can go a long way toward explaining the repeated finding of "revolutionary thought" in *Gargantua and*

Pantagruel (or at least in *Pantagruel*). Such readings of Rabelais's text would themselves be largely "monologistic," of course, in that they single out one aspect or voice in the pluralism, privilege it as the meaning of the author, and ignore the rest. Nonetheless, because the text is open to such diversity, because it is so pluralistic, it can supply those of even antiestablishment beliefs with apparent "Rabelaisian support."

Two distinctions need to be made here, however, before my own argument is appropriated by eager deconstructionists (or readers of Jean Paris). While Rabelais allows a certain pluralism in *Pantagruel*, it is not true that he includes (or associates and fails to condemn) conflicting views ("voices") on every point treated in the narrative. Though I cannot prove this here, I do firmly believe that Rabelais's first text can be—and is—quite "monologistic" at times. In other words, I believe that one can construct valid monologistic interpretations of this novel, its parts or its entirety, without one's work being rightfully subject to blanket dismissals like "But the very text is pluralistic! What right have you to privilege any one voice or voices as the voice(s) of the text?" In short, I do not believe that the occasional pluralism of *Pantagruel* invalidates monologistic interpretations of all kinds.

Second, there is a definite shift in the pluralism of *Gargantua and Pantagruel* from the first to the second novel, at least as regards *Utopia*. Whereas Rabelais in his first novel gives the name "Utopie" to Gargantua and Pantagruel's kingdom, using the word (often quite prominently) six times in the course of the text, as well as drawing several other names from More's work, in *Gargantua* all references to *Utopia* vanish. Not once does Rabelais refer to Grandgousier and Gargantua's land of residence as "Utopie"; indeed, when mentioning surrounding towns and villages he always employs names of real places in Touraine. Thus, while he never actually states that his giants no longer reside in Utopie (which lay somewhere east of India), he does everything possible to suggest that their land is now in the heart of France. Never does he draw place names or other terms from More's work in his second novel.

There are several possible reasons, in addition to Lefranc's old hypothesis that with the Picrocholine War Rabelais sought to lampoon his father's Tourangeau neighbor, and enemy, Gaucher de Ste. Marthe.[6] In 1532, at the time Rabelais wrote *Pantagruel*, Sir Thomas More was still a respected, and universally respectable, lord chancellor of England. Shortly thereafter, however, he quarreled with Henry VIII over the latter's ecclesiastical dealings and finally resigned his post. Henry had him charged with high treason when he refused to endorse the divorce from Catherine of Aragon or deny the pope's authority in church affairs, and by 1534 More was sent to the Tower of London. The next year, still unrepentant, he was beheaded.

As this rather rapid change in his fortunes should suggest, while mention of Sir Thomas More would have been relatively unproblematic (especially in France) in 1532, it would have been highly indiscreet in 1534 (or 1535), by which time More, despite his allegiance to the Catholic church, had become an internationally known example of a subject's defiance of his king. On these grounds alone, and particularly when considered in conjunction with the greatly increased respect for authority in *Gargantua* brought out in Part II, Section 1, above, it would hardly be surprising if Rabelais should have chosen to put as much distance as possible between himself, his text, and Erasmus's "man for all seasons."[7]

Nonetheless, at least for the duration of the first novel, *Gargantua and Pantagruel* is indeed pluralistic and "polyphonic" (in Bakhtin's sense of the term). I am sure that, had he not been otherwise preoccupied, Bakhtin could have brought this pluralism out when he turned to write on Rabelais. Certainly his work on Dostoevsky proves that he was attuned to such matters. Indeed, if I have found such pluralism in Rabelais's text, it is because Bakhtin's *Dostoevsky* caused me to be aware of and look for such elements. It is for this reason that I can very honestly say that I offer this analysis as my homage to Mikhail Bakhtin the literary critic and theorist.

Conclusion

And that is what I have to say, for the moment at least, about Bakhtin's *Rabelais*, Rabelais and popular culture, and Bakhtin's usefulness in understanding Rabelais. As I hope to have shown, the function and position of popular culture in *Gargantua and Pantagruel* is by no means the unchanging, completely dominant monolith described by Mikhail Bakhtin. In *Pantagruel* popular culture operates on a par with, but not to the exclusion of, learned culture. In *Gargantua* one can watch Rabelais exclude it from his narrative, until, with the *Third Book*, he shuts it out almost entirely. As of the *Fourth Book* the author allows popular culture back into his narrative to a limited extent, but often with negative connotations and almost never in association with his figures of power and authority. There is a certain "loosening up" in the *Fourth Book* on the part of the narrator but nothing approaching a return to the values and manners of the first narrative. Yet if Bakhtin's interpretation of *Gargantua and Pantagruel* is not a valid presentation of François Rabelais's actual text, this is not to say that Bakhtin's own work is valueless in approaching at least the first of Rabelais's narratives.

Though I criticize Bakhtin's description and interpretation of Rabelais's text, I do not argue the validity of one of his main theses and theoretical foundations: that one can escape the conceptual "prison-house" of any one cultural (as for instance, dominant-class) ideology, get outside it and its language, view it objectively, and criticize it by juxtaposing its discourse to the discourse of another ideology (such as that of popular culture). Bakhtin may very well be right on this point.

Yet the validity of this thesis does not seem particularly relevant to an analysis of *Gargantua and Pantagruel*, since, after *Pantagruel*, Rabelais does not employ popular culture in a fashion, or to an extent, that allows for any such self-distancing from, much less criticism of, dominant-class culture from a popular-culture perspective. To be rather blunt, the validity of Bakhtin's theoretical basis is not relevant to a discussion of *Gargantua and Pantagruel* because, after *Pantagruel*, there is no longer any real cultural (or, to use Bakhtin's term, "linguistic") pluralism.

Such self-distancing and even criticism is indeed present in the first narrative. Given the contemporary status of popular culture with the dominant classes, however, and the fact that this criticism is not taken up again in the later narratives, even this criticism cannot necessarily be interpreted as intentionally hostile or external. In other words, even when there is cultural ("linguistic") pluralism in Rabelais's text, it does not appear that Rabelais took advantage of it or arranged it to convey—or stimulate in his readers—anything like the antiestablishment criticism and hostility ascribed to him by Bakhtin.

It would appear, rather, that one of the historical points Bakhtin missed, and one that would have made his interpretation of Rabelais far more valid (though very different), is the fact that during the first part of the sixteenth century the dominant classes themselves enjoyed a cultural plurality that provided them (through popular culture) with a rather considerable self-critical perception. Only with the subsequent exclusion of popular culture from their world did these dominant classes lose this self-critical vision. How strongly—if at all—they felt the hostility directed against them by the people I would not venture to say, but the fact remains that, until they began to exclude aspects of popular culture from their own world, the dominant classes were at least conscious of such a critique. They may well not have taken it particularly seriously, until popular outbreaks and uprisings in the first part of the sixteenth century caused them to do otherwise, but it would have given them a latitude of self-perception that Bakhtin argues for Rabelais and his readers—and denies completely to these dominant classes. Bakhtin may well be right about the conceptual advantages of the simultaneous presence of two distinct cultural ("linguistic") discourses, but he seems to have been very wrong about who experienced these advantages and what their effect was.

Or, as I have said to fervent Bakhtinians more than once, Bakhtin would have been far better off had he kept his attention on "dialogic" writers of a later era, an era that really experienced the cultural segregation that Bakhtin so anachronistically tries to impose upon the first part of the sixteenth century.

I would like to conclude this book with a few extremely general observations on the "greater historical context" of my subject matter.

One of the things that has most fascinated me about the sixteenth century is the general shift from heterogeneity to homogeneity that seems to mark so many of the cultural aspects of the era. The most obvious instance of this shift would certainly be in the case of organized religion. By the end of the Middle Ages, Western Europe had only one major organized religion. Within its boundaries, late medieval Roman Catholicism tolerated a relative diversity of theological viewpoints. There were certainly limits past which one could not proceed without expulsion and punishment, as Johann Hus and others accused of heresy discovered. The fact remained, however, that even as late as 1500, organized Christianity in Western Europe was a definitely pluralistic domain.

With the development of the various Protestant faiths during the sixteenth century, this pluralistic atmosphere within organized Christianity was considerably reduced. It is certainly true, of course, that with the Reformation there came about a diversity of organized Christian religions previously unknown. Luther, and especially Calvin, developed "rational" theologies, however: systems of belief (at least presented as) logically derived from one or two basic tenets. Unlike medieval Catholicism, these faiths were under no constraint to encompass anything like the corpus of writings of many often divergent Catholic Church Fathers. As a result, they could be more "rational," "ordered." The Protestant faiths consequently provided little or no room for divergent or contradictory stances. Though there was now a diversity of Christian religions, these "new" religions were each, in themselves, far less doctrinally diverse than the faith from which they had broken away.

Even Roman Catholicism became less pluralistic by the end of the sixteenth century. Confronted with the criticism of the various Reformers, the Roman Catholic church was also caught up in an effort to justify itself. This involved, at least to a certain extent, attempts to define and to rationally order its doctrines. As a result, by 1600 the Roman Catholic church displayed considerably less doctrinal heterogeneity than had existed within its realm a century before.

The change in the nature of "upper-class" culture described in the preceding study was in many ways structurally similar to the contemporary changes in organized Christian religion. In 1500, these upper classes enjoyed a definite cultural pluralism, participating in both learned and popular culture. Yet by 1600 these upper classes no longer tolerated such heterogeneity, in part because they felt a need to define themselves as different from "the people," as the Roman Catholic church had felt the need to define itself as different and distinct from the Protestant faiths. The upper-class cultural realm, now deprived of its popular component, became, like the doctrine of organized Christian religion, far more homogeneous, less heterogeneous.

This same "weeding out," "paring down," ordering and systematizing, can also be seen in the treatment of Latin. During the Middle Ages, Latin had developed a wide range of possibilities and alternatives. Such heterogeneity was rejected during the Renaissance, however, as emphasis was placed upon maintaining a "purer," more "classical" discourse (whether Ciceronian or Erasmian). There was now far greater limitation on the range of possibilities.

The same shift from heterogeneity to homogeneity can be observed over and over again in various other facets of "upper-class" Western European culture during this period. Whereas in the Late Middle Ages a given group (the Roman Catholic church, the nobility, writers of Latin) had accepted a certain heterogeneity, a range of possibilities and potentials, during the sixteenth century that same group restricted its range of operations, its choices and options.

Here, in this sea of great historical generalizations, I would not dare to throw out an explanation. (Though I will hazard a warning: Max Weber's talk of the "rationalization of labor" tied to the now-infamous "Protestant work ethic" is chronologically out of place in the sixteenth century, and so should not be brought up here as a facile solution.) Rather, I am perfectly content to have pointed out, even if only in the most general and unsophisticated way, that the change in dominant-class culture which occurred in France during the first part of the sixteenth century, a change which figures and plays a role in *Gargantua and Pantagruel*, was itself only part of a much broader transformation that was manifested in different ways by different aspects of Western European learned culture. For some reason or reasons, the upper classes, both in general and in particular segments, chose to eliminate existing diversities, pluralisms, heterogeneities, from various aspects of their life.

The result, in part, was the "classicism" of the seventeenth century—obviously a strictly upper-class development. But the heritage of that shift continues to exert its effects in many ways on Western culture down to the present.

Nowhere is this truer than in much—indeed, most—Western literary criticism. As a result, the shift of the sixteenth century must be kept in mind when we, who come after it, deal with the writings of "pre-shift" authors like Rabelais. We must remember that the complexity and diversity of his narratives cannot be treated as a product of our "post-shift," homogeneity-oriented mentality. Though it is perfectly valid (in my opinion) to bring out individual systems and structures in *Gargantua and Pantagruel*, these coherent, rational systems must always be seen as part of the extremely complex, heterogeneous whole. Indeed, one might even question the validity of applying to Rabelais's texts any sort of Goldmannian "genetic structuralism" or other approach predicated on the assumption (derived from nineteenth-century developments in biology) that a work of art is the elaboration of some one, basic, "deep" pattern or structure.

Comparisons from one art to another are often deceptively appealing, but it might be worth recalling along these lines that Rabelais's narratives are structurally the contemporaries, and perhaps the literary equivalents, of pre-single-point perspective painting. While it would certainly appear justifiable to search for and highlight aspects of *Gargantua and Pantagruel* that allow for the explanation of several individual moments as a function of one more general pattern, the critic and the reader must be very leery of any attempt to suggest that the works themselves are elaborations of any one "unifying," "generating" principle or structure. Like any other author, Rabelais has to be approached on his own terms. But these terms may involve some reexamination of our own critical methodologies and their underlying assumptions.

Notes

PREFACE

1 Mireille Huchon has argued convincingly that the work known for the last four centuries as *The Fifth Book of Pantagruel* is in fact an (apparently unauthorized) agglomeration of sketches that Rabelais had written for the *Third* and *Fourth Books* and then rejected. See Mireille Huchon, *Rabelais grammairien*, Etudes Rabelaisiennes, 16 (Geneva: Droz, 1981), 412–89. In the light of Ms. Huchon's argument, the *Fifth Book* would actually appear to be "authentic," in that the text was originally from Rabelais's hand (or at least most of it; Huchon believes that several chapters were added to Rabelais's sketches posthumously by those who put the sketches together and published them as a *Fifth Book*). Since, however, Rabelais's sketches may have been subject to an unknown amount of alteration by the posthumous compilers, it would seem best to exclude the *Fifth Book* from the present attempt to reconstruct the development of Rabelais's thoughts on popular culture from 1532 to 1552.

PART I

1 *Rabelais and His World*, trans. Helene Iswolsky (Cambridge: MIT Press, 1968); *L'Oeuvre de François Rabelais et la culture populaire au Moyen Age et sous la Renaissance*, trans. Andrée Robel (Paris: Gallimard, 1970); *La Cultura popular en la Edad Media y Renacimiento* (Barcelona: Berral, 1974); *L'Opera di Rabelais e la cultura popular; riso, carnevale e*

festa nella tradizione medievale e rinascimentale (Turin: Einaudi, 1979). *Literatur und Karnival zur Romantheorie und Lachkultur* (Munich: Hanser, 1969), is apparently a translation of only part of the text.

2 Michel Beaujour, *Le jeu de Rabelais* (Paris: L'Herne, 1969), 8–9.

3 Among recent journal special issues devoted to Bakhtin are *Critical Inquiry* 10, no. 2 (December 1983), and *Studies in Twentieth Century Literature* 9, no. 1 (Fall 1984).

4 Etienne Gilson, "Rabelais franciscain," in *Les Idées et les lettres* (Paris: Vrin, 1932), 197–241; Jean Plattard, "L'Ecriture sainte et la littérature scripturaire dans l'oeuvre de Rabelais," *Revue des Etudes Rabelaisiennes* 8 (1910): 257–330, and 9 (1911): 423–36.

5 On the history of Bakhtin's *Rabelais*, see Katerina Clark and Michael Holquist's fascinating *Mikhail Bakhtin* (Cambridge: Harvard University Press, 1984).

6 On the history of Rabelais's "image," see Marcel de Grève, *L'Interprétation de Rabelais au XVIe siècle*, Etudes Rabelaisiennes, 3 (Geneva: Droz, 1961), and Jacques Boulenger, *Rabelais à travers les âges* (Paris: Le Divan, 1925).

7 Lefranc's prefaces have been reprinted in Lefranc, *Rabelais* (Paris: Albin Michel, 1953).

8 See, for example Jean Plattard's remarks in his *Life of François Rabelais*, trans. Louis P. Roche (New York: Alfred Knopf, 1931), 292: "Contemporary criticism no longer regards Rabelais as 'an abyss of the mind' or a prodigious thinker. . . . It would seem to place a lesser value on Rabelais' thought, which is not always original, than on his qualities as an artist."

9 Lucien Febvre, *Le Problème de l'incroyance au 16e siècle: La Religion de Rabelais* (Paris: Albin Michel, 1942; rpt. 1968), translated into English by Beatrice Gottlieb as *The Problem of Unbelief in the Sixteenth Century: The Religion of Rabelais* (Cambridge: Harvard University Press, 1982).

10 "Charm" struck me as the wrong word here, so I checked the French translation. "Charm" and the entire paragraph in which it figures are absent from the French version, which has a completely different paragraph in its place. See *L'Oeuvre de François Rabelais*, 67.

11 What, one might or should ask, are Bakhtin's sources, his basis for so extensive and elaborate a description of popular culture? One will have to keep on asking, I'm afraid. Bakhtin indicates very few primary sources, and one often has the impression that his "medieval

and Renaissance popular culture" is largely an amalgamation of Goethe's notes on an eighteenth-century Venetian carnival and Bakhtin's own preconception of what that popular culture should have been. But see also Part III of this study.

12 "Monolingual" is used figuratively here, of course. For Bakhtin, all "official" languages—"official" French, "official" English, etc.— would have been the same in this respect, in that they all conveyed the same official culture and/or ideology. For Bakhtin, a sixteenth-century individual who spoke half a dozen such languages might have been every bit as intellectually shackled as someone who knew only one. Such would be the case of the Thelemites, who are all multilingual, though not of the *Pantagruel* Panurge of chapter 9, who mixes popular and learned culture in several different languages and introduces popular culture elements under the guise of "invented" languages. "Mono-cultural" might be a better word.

13 One question raised by his interpretation that Bakhtin never confronts is, For whom did Rabelais write? I.e., whom was he trying to liberate from linguistic dogmatism? Bakhtin does once refer to *Gargantua and Pantagruel* as "mass literature" (B 157), but he doesn't stress the point; even in 1940 it was widely known that the percentage of the "masses" who could read—or afford a book—during Rabelais's time was very small. Nor is *Gargantua and Pantagruel* likely to have been written for that small minority of literate "proletariat"; the work's classical references and legal and medical citations make this quite clear. (On this point, one has only to compare even the first of Rabelais's narratives to the *Grandes et inestimables cronicques* from which it was derived; Rabelais's book would have been far less accessible to the "masses" than its source.)

On the other hand, and despite the opening lines of the *Pantagruel* Prologue, *Gargantua and Pantagruel* was most likely not aimed at the nobility. Nasier may speak to "most illustrious and most chivalric champions, noblemen, and others" (167; *P* 3), but when he tells his readers not to think about their "trade" (*mestier*) (167; *P* 4), it is obvious that he is addressing, not nobles, but men who work for a living. In his recent article, "The First Edition of *Pantagruel*," *Etudes Rabelaisiennes* 15 (1980): 31–42, M. A. Screech has shown that the first edition of *Pantagruel* had as its frontispiece a plate that was normally used for legal works. Though Rabelais may have seen his audience expand with time, he seems to have written *Gargantua and*

Pantagruel for people like himself and his friends (lawyers, doctors, etc.), people who could understand his allusions to legal, medical, and classical texts, but who were nevertheless "working men," men who knew what it meant to face poverty and who could appreciate—and had experienced—the inequities of the sociopolitical structure.

14 It should be noted, in all fairness to Bakhtin, that the systematic, scientific study of medieval and Renaissance popular culture is a very recent development in historiography. We now know far more about the culture of this period than Bakhtin could have learned from secondary sources in the thirties and forties, or even in the sixties.

PART II

1. *The Presence and Exclusion of Popular Culture in* Pantagruel *and* Gargantua

1 As Yves-Marie Bercé has shown, writing and books were regarded as foreign and threatening in popular culture throughout the sixteenth century and well after. In that respect, Alcofribas Nasier, who repeatedly talks about the books he has already written or intends to write, is very much a part of learned culture even in *Pantagruel*.

2 The exact year of the first edition of *Gargantua*—1535, 1534, or even earlier—is still subject to dispute. I myself am convinced by the arguments that place the publication of the novel in 1535, but the question is not particularly relevant to this study. On this point the interested reader can consult the following: Gérard Defaux, "Les Dates de composition et de publication du *Gargantua*: Essai de mise en point," *Etudes Rabelaisiennes* 11 (1974): 137–42; M. A. Screech, "Some Reflexions on the Problem of Dating 'Gargantua A' and 'B'," ibid., 9–56; Marcel Françon, "Note sur la datation de *Gargantua*," ibid., 81–82; M. A. Screech, "Some Further Reflexions on the Dating of *Gargantua* (A) and (B) and on the Possible Meaning of Some of the Episodes," ibid. 13 (1976): 79–111; and Mireille Huchon, *Rabelais grammairien*, Etudes Rabelaisiennes, 16 (Geneva: Droz, 1981), 111–13.

3 This passage was added in the second 1535 edition.

4 Further examples: To substantiate his opinion concerning the supremacy of his favorite arse-wipe, Gargantua refers to the "heroes

and demigods in the Elysian Fields" and cites "Master Duns Scotus" (69; *G* 93); to express his pleasure with Gargantua's new-found interest in personal hygiene, Grandgousier recounts an anecdote about Philip of Macedonia and Alexander (69–70; *G* 94–95); to support his claims for the size of Gargantua's mare's tail, Nasier mentions "the tail of the Scythian rams . . . [and] of the Syrian sheep" (73; *G* 104); to describe Ponocrates' and Eudemon's laughter after they listen to Janotus de Bragmardo, Nasier recites an anecdote about Crassus and Philemon (79; *G* 124); to convey Gargantua's athletic prowess, Nasier refers to Julius Caesar, Stentor, and Milo (90–91; *G* 153). In each case learned culture is called upon to the exclusion of popular culture, even though the subject matter itself—arse-wipes, horses' tails, etc.—would often seem to lend itself more to the latter than the former.

5 Michel Psichari, "Les Jeux de Gargantua," *Revue des Etudes Rabelaisiennes* 6 (1908): 1–37, 174–81, 317–61.

6 Alban J. Krailsheimer, *Rabelais and the Franciscans* (Oxford: Clarendon Press, 1963), 3–90.

7 This passage may have been suggested to Rabelais by an episode in the *Grandes et inestimables cronicques* in which Gargantua, attacked by the army of the king of Ireland and Holland, caught up many of the soldiers "and filled the bottom of his breeches with them" (*Cronicques* 122). One of these prisoners is subsequently killed "by the wind of a fart that Gargantua made in his breeches" (ibid.). The anonymous author then goes on to explain that Gargantua "farted so strongly, that he made three wagon-loads of hay overturn with the wind that came out of his body, and with a poop he made four windmills grind" (122–23). If I have quoted this passage at length, it is because it is the only excremental passage in all of the *Grandes et inestimables cronicques*—and even then, there is not really a question of excrement except by association. In general, popular culture (as Bakhtin and, to an extent, I am defining it) is almost entirely absent from the *Grandes et inestimables cronicques*.

8 This is after the young giant comes under the tutelage of Ponocrates. Before that, but after Chapter 14, it seems that Gargantua made use of a chamber-pot (83; *G* 133), which would most likely have been kept inside the living quarters.

9 With one apparent qualification, or distinction: after chapter 14, solid excretions are taken care of out of sight, but such is not always the case with urine. Having climbed a tower of Notre-Dame Cathe-

dral (chap. 17), Gargantua "undid his magnificent codpiece and, bringing out his tool, pissed on them [the Parisians] so freely that he drowned two hundred and sixty thousand, four hundred and eighteen persons, not counting the women and small children" (74; *G* 107). During the Picrocholine War, Gargantua's mare relieves herself, making a flood twenty-one miles wide that drowns many of the enemy soldiers (117; *G* 209). Having finished a celebratory banquet, Gargantua goes outside to "piss away my misfortune. . . . So copiously did he piss indeed that his urine cut the pilgrims' road" (122; *G* 219). There is definitely a "distinction of objectionability" made between feces and urine as of *Gargantua*. See also the discussion of the changing perception and use of excrement during the sixteenth century in Natalie Z. Davis's fascinating *Society and Culture in Early Modern France* (Stanford: Stanford University Press, 1975), 180ff.

10 In fact, on this point of excretion, Rabelais actually went back and toned down certain passages in *Pantagruel*—something he seldom did. In the first edition of the narrative, the dogs "shat all over [the great Parisian lady] and pissed over all her clothes" (*la conchioient toute et compissoyent tous ses habillemens*) (244; *P* 124). As of the 1542 François Juste edition, they simply urinate on her clothes (cf. *Pantagruel*, ed. Abel Lefranc et al., 1: 242, note to line 50). In the first edition, Pantagruel is depicted as so involved in trying to understand the dispute of Baisecul and Humevesne that he "farted with much effort" (*petoit d'ahan*) (212; *P* 72). These words are excised after the 1533 François Juste edition.

11 As usual, Bakhtin provides no documentation for his assertions.

12 Since the one extant copy of the first edition of *Gargantua* is missing its title page, on the back of which this *dizain* would have appeared if it was included in that edition, we now have no way of knowing whether this poem was included in the first edition of the novel. It is present as of the second 1535 edition.

13 To be more precise, one should say that this rejection occurs within, rather than with, *Gargantua*. Though those afflicted with venereal disease are excluded from Theleme, and though disease has only negative connotations in the course of the narrative, the *Gargantua* Prologue begins, "Most noble boozers, and you my very esteemed and poxy friends [*verolés*]—for to you and you alone are my writings dedicated" (37; *G* 9). As with excrement, so with disease, rejection seems to occur in the course of the narration. (For this reason, one might argue that the liminary *dizain* did *not* appear at the opening of

the first edition of the novel, or at least that it was not written until after the completion of the work. See the preceding note.)

14 In subsequent editions, the first chapter also recounts the origin of "balls of Lorraine, which never stay in a codpiece" (172; *P* 12), and adds to the simple mention of the giant Gayoffe the information that his "balls were of poplar and his prick of sorb-apple wood" (173; *P* 14).

15 François Rabelais, *Oeuvres complètes*, ed. Pierre Jourda (Paris: Garnier, 1962), 1:294, n. 2. Cohen translates it as "the Gobelin pleasure-house."

16 A somewhat more outspoken student of mine once referred to Panurge as a "sex maniac." The description is accurate, whether or not one accepts the moral condemnation that the student certainly meant to express with it.

17 In the *Grandes et inestimables cronicques*, King Arthur rewards Gargantua with a suit of his livery for defeating the armies of Gos and Magos (114). But then, as already mentioned, the *Grandes et inestimables cronicques* are almost entirely lacking in aspects of popular culture.

18 As with farts, so this braguette—and, by implication and quite logically, the organ inside it—is associated with life itself. In preparing Epistemon's severed head to be rejoined to his body, Panurge "took the head and held it over his codpiece" (265; *P* 159).

19 The difference between Gargantua and Pantagruel in this same situation very much recalls the difference between Odysseus' reaction when he learns of Elpenor's death and Aeneas' reaction when he discovers that Palinurus has died. Odysseus returns to Circe's island to give Elpenor a proper burial, even though it means delaying his voyage home, whereas Aeneas sails on in fulfillment of his duty to the future state of Rome, leaving Palinurus' body without proper funeral rites. Just as Vergil played off Homer's text to develop Aeneas through contrast, so Rabelais would seem to refer back to *Pantagruel* in order to show by contrast how different Gargantua has become.

20 Panurge's power and authority in *Pantagruel* are illustrated below, and developed at length in Gérard Defaux's *Pantagruel et les sophistes* (The Hague: Martinus Nijhoff, 1973).

21 In the 1542 François Juste edition, he precedes this question with another: "Isn't it a jolly death, to die with a stiff john-thomas?" (123; *G* 223).

22 In general, Rabelais seems to have transferred Gargantua's early sexu-

ality to Friar John, which brings to mind Defaux's demonstration, in *Pantagruel et les sophistes*, of how Rabelais transferred Pantagruel's early sophistry to Panurge in the later chapters of *Pantagruel*.

23 So, at least, Louis Marin proposed, in his "Les Corps utopiques rabelaisiens," *Littérature* 21 (1975): 35–51. The question is more complicated than Marin's article would suggest, however. It is quite true that at one point the narrator says, "When the time came that anyone in that abbey, either at his parents' request or for any other reason, wished to leave it, he took with him one of the ladies, the one who had accepted him as her admirer, and they were married to one another; and if at Theleme they had lived in devotion and friendship, they lived in still greater devotion and friendship when they were married" (160; *G* 304). Since these couples get married only after they leave the abbey, it might be inferred that there are no married couples in Theleme—though of course there can be sex without marriage, and the phrase "devotion and friendship" (*devotion et amityé*) *might* suggest that such is the case in Theleme. Earlier in his description of the abbey, however, the narrator had remarked: "Because ordinarily monks and nuns made three vows, that is of chastity, poverty, and obedience, it was decreed that there [in Theleme] anyone could be regularly married, could become rich, and could live at liberty" (151; *G* 283–84). Here it is quite clear that marriages—and hence, one would suppose, sex—are allowed in Theleme, and celebacy is not required or expected.

24 Though Bakhtin asserted that "the significance of banquet images is considerable in all the legends about giants (for instance, in the Gargantua story and in the chapbook relating it, which were the direct source of Rabelais' novel)" (B 297), he is wrong concerning the *Cronicques*. That work contains only one banquet, arranged by King Arthur to celebrate Gargantua's defeat of the Gos and Magos. The young giant is presented with a wonderful abundance of foodstuffs but is evidently not invited to join in the noble conversation. The narrator remarks: "Gargantua took his meal . . . while listening to [not "joining in"] the fine words and honest games and sayings of the King and the princes who were in attendance there" (116). (Note the "fine words" and "honest games and sayings," rather than "free and jocular speech".) As has already been remarked, the *Cronicques* are almost entirely devoid of elements of popular culture. They also support without question the absolute authority of monarchs over their subjects; Gargantua is always treated as—and seems quite happy to

be—a glorified servant of King Arthur, whom he always addresses with great respect and self-humbling deference.

Robert Muchambled has argued that in the sixteenth century popular legends were often published by the "establishment" in "co-opted" versions "redesigned" to inculcate establishment ideology in the "people." Though I have no idea what the "original," "folk" version of the Gargantua story was like—how can we ever know if all we have to deal with are written, published "versions"?—the *Cronicques* seem a fine proof text for Muchambled's argument.

25 R. H. Armitage, "Is *Gargantua* a Reworking of *Pantagruel* I?" *PMLA* 59 (1944): 944–51.

26 This explanation has been offered by so distinguished a Rabelais scholar as M. A. Screech, in "Some Reflexions on the Abbey of Thelema," *Etudes Rabelaisiennes* 8 (1969): 109–14.

27 On the editions of *Gargantua* published during the author's lifetime and Rabelais's involvement in them, see Huchon, *Rabelais grammairien*, 106–10.

28 Cf. Gérard Defaux, "Rabelais et son masque comique: *Sophista loquitur*," *Etudes Rabelaisiennes* 11 (1974): 89–136.

29 Cf. Richard M. Berrong, "*Gargantua* and the New Historiography," *University of Dayton Review* 16, no. 3 (Winter 1983–84): 47–54.

30 This quatrain first appeared in François Juste's 1534 edition. (Though Saulnier's edition of *Pantagruel* indicates passages that Rabelais added in subsequent editions, it does not specify in what edition a given passage first appeared. For this information, the best edition to consult is still the one prepared by Abel Lefranc and his circle, known as the *édition magistrale*, published in two volumes by Champion [Paris, 1922].)

31 "Take no care for his trade" (*ne se souciast de son mestier*) does not appear until the 1542 François Juste edition. (One could argue that this addition indicates the development on the part of the author of a more direct address to, and a clearer awareness of, his "real" audience—perhaps through the experience of seeing who actually bought his books.)

32 As of the 1534 François Juste edition, Nasier closes the novel by re-iterating that he has written it "while passing time" ([*en*] *passant temps*) just as his audience should read it "as a joyous pastime" (*pour passetemps joyeulx*) (*P* 178n). Cohen reduces both of these to "for mere amusement" (277).

33 Burke lists as his source for this poem F. Cottignies, *Chansons et Pas-*

quilles, ed. F. Carton (Arras, 1965), which I have not been able to consult for a precise date—if any is given.

34 The "most illustrious and most valorous champions, noblemen, and others" to whom *Pantagruel* is addressed are described as having been able to "spend their time" with honorable ladies and maidens telling them "fine long stories" from the *Grandes et inestimables cronicques* when they were "hors de propos" ("had nothing else to do," perhaps) (167; *P* 3–4). The narrator tells them that he has written *Pantagruel* "to increase your entertainment" (*passetemps*) (168; *P* 6) and recounts Pantagruel's genealogy "seeing that we have leisure" (171; *P* 9). The understanding of royalty as those who are rich enough not to have to work—in other words, as those who enjoy the ideal life only dreamed of by most men of the era—may explain the positive presentation of and even fascination with nobility that exists in *Pantagruel* concurrent with the critical depiction discussed below. In the passages just quoted above, leisure time is presented as something wonderful and (for Rabelais's real audience) rare. The notion that this book was written for the reader's free time would therefore indicate that it was meant as something special—just as being described as having spare time to read a book would have been almost a form of flattery for Rabelais's readers.

35 The original French—"institué en telle discipline"—is somewhat difficult to translate ("instructed in such a regimen," perhaps), but does not in any way imply that Gargantua is being disciplined, i.e., punished, by Ponocrates.

36 In his fascinating monograph *Les Bourgeois Gentilshommes*, George Huppert cites Gargantua's "second" education as a reflection of the often hectic attempts of the growing French upper middle class to distinguish itself from the rest of the bourgeoisie and liken itself to the nobility by its education and accomplishments. (*Les Bourgeois Gentilshommes* [Chicago: University of Chicago Press, 1977], 83; see chap. 7 on the purpose and function of upper-middle-class "Schools".) This may in fact be the case—though *Gargantua* does date from somewhat before the period in which Huppert shows these efforts to occur—but Gargantua's (and Ponocrates') efforts not to waste even one hour must also be seen as part of a larger condemnation of idleness, demonstrated and analyzed below.

37 Again, of course, this is a change that escaped Bakhtin entirely. I can't say that I am altogether happy to have noticed it myself.

38 Cf., for example, André Biéler, *La Pensée économique et sociale de Jean*

NOTES TO PAGES 46–49   137

Calvin (Geneva: Librairie de l'Université, 1961), or Kurt Samuelsson, *Religion and Economic Action: A Critique of Max Weber* (New York: Harper and Row, 1961).

39 One must be careful to note that this rich/poor dichotomy is not the same as "learned/popular" or Bakhtin's "official/popular." The penurious include anyone without money, such as philosophers, no matter how learned or "official" they might be. As with Nasier's desire to be a king, expressed at the opening of the novel, so here the major difference between men is presented in terms of money: if one doesn't have it, one has to work to stay alive; if one does, one can enjoy that most desired and prized of states, leisure.

40 This is very much Bakhtin's understanding of Carnival, but it has also been advanced by such respectable modern historians as Natalie Z. Davis (*Society and Culture*, chap. 2). The image of an egalitarian society certainly figured prominently in medieval and Renaissance millenarian thought.

41 In *Pantagruel et les sophistes*, Defaux demonstrates the way in which Panurge's humiliation of the great lady and others is part of Rabelais's negative presentation and critique of his era's fascination with dialectic and sophistry. My own interpretation of certain of these instances is not, I believe, incompatible with—and is certainly not meant as a rejection of—Defaux's commentary.

42 By now it should be clear that Pantagruel is often presented as approving of, or at least enjoying, the condemnation or humiliation of "fellow nobles." In this respect, it is interesting to consider one of the changes that Rabelais made from the *Grandes et inestimables cronicques*. In that work, Grantgousier and Gargamelle (Pantagruel's paternal grandparents) are created by Merlin out of whalebone and the blood of Lancelot (for Grantgousier) or the nails of Guinevere (for Gargamelle). As a result, while the giants have no real noble ancestry, they—and hence Gargantua, the main character of the work— are nonetheless at least in part of noble blood. Rabelais scraps this explanation of the giants' origin altogether with his first narrative, replacing it with a long genealogy that links Pantagruel and Gargantua to Adam and his first descendants. In so doing, Rabelais is very clearly underplaying—dare one go so far as to say "denying"?—any connection between royalty as he and his readers knew it and the royal family of his fictional Utopie. In other words, if Pantagruel laughs at and is not offended by the humiliation of the great Parisian lady, Humevesne and Baisecul, Anarche, and other artistocrats—not

to mention Panurge's remark about "these accursed kings"—there is no real inconsistency. In *Pantagruel*, unlike in the *Grandes et inestimables cronicques*, the giant has nothing in common with other princes but his title.

43 The *Grandes et inestimables cronicques* opens (105) with an address to "all good knights and noblemen" (*tous bons chevalliers et gentilz hommes*). In this work, unlike in *Pantagruel*, royalty are admired and praised unreservedly throughout. Gargantua spends most of his life very happily in the service of King Arthur (he does not have a kingdom of his own) and derives "one hundred thousand times" more pleasure from listening to "the beautiful words and proper games and devices of the King and the princes who attended the royal banquet" than he does from "drinking or eating" (116). In this respect as well, there is no trace of popular culture, its views and values, in the *Grandes et inestimables cronicques*.

44 Though Picrochole—like Anarche, his homologue in *Pantagruel*—is also humiliated and, again, by "inferiors." During his ignominious flight after losing the last battle, the King of Lerné, having killed his own horse for stumbling, tries to steal an ass: "But the millers rained blows upon him, stripped him of his clothes, and gave him a wretched smock to cover him. . . . No one knows what has become of him since then. All the same I have been told that at present he is a miserable porter at Lyons" (144; *G* 270).

45 Rabelais did not go back and alter the genealogy he had constructed in *Pantagruel* so as to reconnect Gargantua, as of *Gargantua*, with some recognized earthly nobility, but he does mention that Grandgousier wanted his son to wear certain rings "in order to revive this old mark of nobility" (57; *G* 62).

46 He did go out of his way. Ponocrates' death, and the mention of it, serve no function in the narrative. It is never referred to or made use of elsewhere.

2. *The Historical Context of Rabelais's Changing
Attitude toward Popular Culture*

1 Several historians have noted the development of a definitely sharper distinction between sacred and profane during the sixteenth century. See Muchambled 209; Burke 211.

2 On this phenomenon, see George Huppert, *Les Bourgeois Gentils-hommes* (Chicago: University of Chicago Press, 1977).

3 The chronological coincidence of *Gargantua* (1534/35) with the events at Münster has always intrigued me. Despite considerable effort, however, I have never been able to demonstrate any real link between the Lerneans' capture of La Roche Clermaud and the Ana-baptists' seizure of Münster. Closer to home—for Rabelais—one might note the "Grande Rebeine," a major uprising in Lyons in 1529 during which a mob, mainly of the poor, ransacked the local Franciscan monastery and the homes of notables (Knecht 314–15). Even before *Pantagruel*, Rabelais would have been aware of the dangers posed by an increasingly discontented "people."

4 As R. J. Knecht reports (315), this fear of the unemployed peasant became so great that, in 1537, Francis I empowered anyone to kill roving vagabonds as rebels against the government's authority. There may be just the slightest indication of this fear in the later pages of *Gargantua*, where the title character, near the end of his address to the vanquished Lerneans, promises the captured troops that "you shall be safely escorted [back to Lerné] by six-hundred men-at-arms and eight thousand foot under the command of my squire Alexan-der, *so that you shall not be molested by the peasants*" (147; *G* 275; my italics). Earlier in the narrative, when Toucquedillon left Grand-gousier to return to Picrochole, the narrator had remarked that "Gargantua gave him an escort of thirty men-at-arms and a hundred and twenty archers under Gymnaste's command, to take him safely to the gates of La Roche Clermault, if need be" (139–40; *G* 261). Here there is no indication of what or whom Toucquedillon needed to be kept safe from.

5 In *Culture and Society in Renaissance Italy (1420–1540)* (New York: Charles Scribner's, 1972), 30–31, Burke refers to such changes as occurring in Italy as early as the fifteenth century.

6 The "standard" biography, Jean Plattard's *François Rabelais* (several editions and versions in French), published in English as *The Life of François Rabelais*, trans. Louis P. Roche [New York: Alfred Knopf, 1931]), contains most of what little we do know about the man, but also a great deal of completely unsupported hypothesis and specula-tion. The documented facts of Rabelais's life can be found in the first chapter of Georges Lote's *La Vie et l'oeuvre de François Rabelais* (Paris: Droz, 1938), since which little has been discovered. (Except, per-

haps, the date of Rabelais's death. See Jean Dupèbe, "La Date de la mort de Rabelais?" *Bibliothèque d'Humanisme et Renaissance* 42, no. 3 [1980]: 657.) M. A. Screech's most recent book on Rabelais, entitled simply *Rabelais* (Ithaca: Cornell University Press, 1979), 462–77, contains a handy chronology.

7 In his study *Rabelais, ses voyages en Italie, son exil à Metz* (Paris: Librairie de l'Art, 1891), 23–24, Arthur Heulhard maintains that du Bellay chose Rabelais less for his medical skills than because he saw in the physician an "authority in all matters of theology and canon law." This is almost certainly an exaggeration of Rabelais's position and importance in du Bellay's retinue. Never once in his published correspondence from this period does du Bellay so much as mention Rabelais. On the other hand, he twice refers to his poor health: indeed, it seems to have been rather bad, since on 8 February he wrote to Louis de Perreau that he could not even bear to be carried in a sedan chair (*La Correspondance du Cardinal Jean du Bellay*, ed. Rémy Scheurer [Paris: Klincksieck, 1969], 1:344, 351). There is therefore good reason to believe that du Bellay felt the need for an attendant physician, and none whatsoever to suppose that he chose Rabelais as a consultant to help him with his negotiations (he was trying to obtain papal consent for Henry VIII's divorce from Catherine of Aragon).

8 Heulhard, *Rabelais*, 92.

9 Indeed, even in the 1490s many Italian nobles found the behavior of Charles VIII's translated court to be shocking and "barbarian"—an indication of how far ahead Italy was in the change of upper-class manners and life-style. On the other hand, Charles, and after him his successors, Louis XII and Francis I, took a great deal of what they found in Italy back to the French royal court with them.

10 On this point, one could cite many passages from the *Colloquies*, such as the following: a student is instructed to pretend that he does not understand if he hears a dirty joke (21; 162); another student says that, when reading poetry (presumably classical) he skips the indecent parts (40; 180); Priapus—who figures so prominently in the *Fourth Book* Prologue—is dismissed as "filthy" (50; 234); a dinner guest remarks, "I disagree with those who think a dinner party isn't fun unless it overflows with silly, bawdy stories and rings with dirty songs," and adds, "True gaiety comes from a clean, sincere conscience" (56; 241); a Carthusian monk—so unlike the narrator and

other characters in *Pantagruel*—berates a soldier who has contracted venereal disease (132–33; 318–19). Indeed, an entire later colloquy—"A Marriage in Name Only"—is devoted to condemning the effects of venereal disease on marriage (401–12; 591–600).

11 This paragraph only barely suggests the tip of what I believe to be a very important aspect of the development of fictional narrative during the sixteenth century. I hope to elaborate on this idea, using Cervantes, Boiardo, Ariosto, and others, in a future monograph. The classic essay on Rabelais's innovative mixing of styles, tones, levels of discourse, and the like and how he differed from his literary predecessors in doing so, remains Erich Auerbach's "The World in Pantagruel's Mouth," in *Mimesis*, trans. Willard R. Trask (Princeton: Princeton University Press, 1971), 262–84.

12 Rabelais's Latin dedicatory epistle can be found in Pierre Jourda's edition of the writer's *Oeuvres complètes* (Paris: Garnier, 1962), 2:525–28, followed by a French translation (529–32). It is not included in Cohen's English edition of the novels, but a translation of it can be found in *The Works of François Rabelais*, ed. Albert J. Nock and Catherine R. Wilson (New York: Harcourt, Brace, 1931), 2:905–7.

13 The earliest French translations did not appear until 1537–38. Although we have no real indication of Rabelais's competency in Italian, we can cite, in addition to the time he spent south of the Alps, the royal privilege granted for the publication of the *Third Book*, dated 1545, in which there is mention that Rabelais "had previously handed over to be printed several books: in Greek, Latin, French, and Tuscan" (*TL* 4; the Privilege is not included in Cohen's edition, and I have not been able to find a published English translation). We have no record—much less a copy—of any work by Rabelais in Italian.

14 Rabelais mentions the *Orlando furioso* in the Prologue of *Pantagruel* as of the 1534 François Juste edition (168; *P* 6, note to line 59).

15 At least with reference to the nobles. The one "Rabelaisian" part of the romance—the story of Astolfo, king of the Lombards, and Jocondo Latini, and how they discover that it is impossible to satisfy the insatiable desires of a woman (canto 28)—is recounted by an innkeeper with a "common tongue" (339; 28.1.6), and dismissed by the narrator as "not essential" (339; 28.2.1–2). (But then, why did Ariosto include it, since it certainly is not essential to his "plot lines"? And if he included it, why did he have his narrator dismiss it?

Was it that he himself enjoyed the story and wanted a chance to tell it, but felt that he had to protect himself against what he foresaw as the negative reaction that would be provoked among his potential readers?) "Commoners" in the *Orlando furioso* do not seem to have any scruples about indulging in "free sex" (cf., e.g., the story of Dolinda, Guinevere's maid, canto 5), but the major (i.e., noble) characters are almost all very chaste—if, albeit, sometimes contrary to their own desires. Once Angelica, a principal character in Boiardo's *Orlando innamorato* (to which the *Orlando furioso* was a sequel), begins to sleep with a man to whom she is not married, she almost vanishes from the work, and certainly from the pantheon of important, distinguished characters. The *Orlando furioso* is definitely written for an audience with "refined tastes."

16 Norbert Elias, *The Civilizing Process*, trans. Edmund Jephcott (New York: Urizen Books, 1978), chap. 2, sec. 10.

17 Cf. for example Astolfo's refusal to kill his enemy Caligorante when he finds the latter entangled in a net, since to take advantage of such a situation would suggest that Astolfo was "cowardly" (159; 15.55.6; in the Italian: would cause him to be accused of "viltà").

18 In general, one could say that there is a substitution of excrement for violence in the move from the young Pantagruel to the child Gargantua.

19 Quoted in Lauro Martines, *Power and Imagination: City-States in Renaissance Italy* (New York: Alfred A. Knopf, 1979), 319. My discussion of "la questione della lingua" is taken from his section entitled "The Language Question," 317–22. The standard work on "la questione della lingua" remains Thérèse Labande-Jeanroy's *La Question de la langue en Italie*, Publications de la Faculté des lettres de l'Université de Strasbourg, 27 (Strasbourg and Paris: Istra, 1925).

20 Martines, *Power and Imagination*, 317–18. In canto 46 of his epic romance, Ariosto momentarily leaves the medieval world of knights and fair ladies to sing the praises of Bembo, "who rescued the purity of our gentle idiom from the drabness of common usage [the *volgare uso tetro*] and gave us an example of how it ought to sound [*quale esser dee*, "how it should be"]" (558–59; 46.15.2–4).

21 The most famous work along these lines is, of course, Joachim du Bellay's *Deffence et illustration de la langue françoyse* (1549), itself an adaptation of an Italian work, Sperone Speroni's *Dialogo delle lingue* (Venice, 1542). A position similar to that of Equicola is to be found

less on the question of vocabulary than on that of correct pronunciation and spelling. On this point, see Ferdinand Brunot, *Histoire de la langue française des origines à 1900* (Paris: Armand Colin, 1906), 2:93–123.

22 There is one problematic passage in the Prologue of the *Fifth Book* which may relate to this mid-century dispute. On this point, see Richard M. Berrong, "The *Cinquiesme Livre* and 'La Querelle de la *Deffence*,'" *Etudes Rabelaisiennes* 15 (1980): 145–59.

23 As already pointed out, the *Third* and *Fourth Book*s were dedicated to—and apparently accepted by—members of the French nobility (Margaret of Navarre and Odet de Coligny, respectively). Participants in the learned culture in France, or at least these members of it, evidently never became as insistent as their Italian counterparts upon a totally "folk-free" language—at least not during the sixteenth century.

24 As of the 1534 François Juste edition, Rabelais changed "absurd words" (*motz absurdes*) to *motz espaves*. An *épave* is an abandoned, wrecked ship (hence Cohen's translation "obsolete words"). The Limousin student's mixture of French and bad Latin certainly produces absurd words, but they cannot really be described as *motz espaves*, since they were never in use to begin with. With his condemnation of *motz espaves*, the narrator's comments begin to resemble certain Italians' reasons for not adopting lock, stock, and barrel the antiquated language of Petrarch and Boccaccio.

25 But not of "absurd" or "obsolete" words. Gallet's oration is in standard, if indeed "folk-free," sixteenth-century French. There are no obsolete French words or words forceably—and "unnaturally"—taken over from the Latin.

26 Quoted in Marcel de Grève, *L'Interprétation de Rabelais au XVIe siècle*, Etudes Rabelaisiennes, 3 (Geneva: Droz, 1961), 17.

27 For a very thorough—and highly amusing—description of these early-sixteenth-century French Neo-Latin poets and their "milieu," see pp. 31–100 of Lucien Febvre's *Le Problème de l'incroyance au 16e siècle: La Religion de Rabelais* (Paris: Albin Michel, 1968). Fortunately, this magnificent book is now available in English, as *The Problem of Unbelief in the Sixteenth Century: The Religion of Rabelais*, trans. Beatrice Gottlieb (Cambridge: Harvard University Press, 1982). In this edition, the passage in question can be found on pp. 17–100.

28 For a survey of sixteenth-century reactions to *Gargantua and Pan-*

tagruel, see Grève, *L'Interprétation de Rabelais*. The most famous reaction of the type to which Rabelais seems to be objecting in the
passage here cited is that of Montaigne, who, in book 2, chapter 10
("On Books") of his *Essays*, classes Rabelais's narratives along with
the *Decameron* and Jean Second's once-popular *Basia* as "livres simplement plaisans" (simply pleasant/agreeable/entertaining books).
There have been attempts to make the first essayist's attitude toward
Rabelais seem more complex than would appear to have been the
case. Given his grouping of Rabelais's works with the *Decameron* and
the *Basia*, however, it would seem that, for Montaigne (1) *Gargantua
and Pantagruel* was distinguished primarily by its sexual license, (2)
such books were "plaisans," but (3) they did not have any deeper,
more serious side (they are "simplement plaisans"). Such a judgment may imply a great deal about Montaigne's views regarding the
importance of matters sexual, at least at this stage in his life and
thought; the passage is part of the first version of the essay, which
Villey dates from 1578. Since this is a large topic in Montaigne studies, one that Montaigne scholars have already done much with, and
since the present work is not a study of Montaigne, I shall leave these
implications for others to interpret and develop.

29 Gérard Defaux has suggested that Rabelais may have been alluding to
this experience in the Prologue to the *Third Book*, in which, explaining that he hopes his work will be well received by readers, the narrator recounts a story about a Ptolemy. Returning from a successful
military campaign, this Ptolemy presented his fellow Egyptians with
a slave who was half-white and half-black (the division running ver-
tically). Contrary to Ptolemy's expectations, however, the people dis-
liked the gift: some laughed at it, others found it to be "a loathsome
monster, created by an error of Nature" (285; *TL* 17). It is quite true,
as I shall show, that, with the *Third Book*, Rabelais drastically curtailed his use of popular culture; still, I do not find sufficient grounds
to suggest that the "two-colored slave" might have been meant to
represent specifically the mixture of learned and popular cultures
in *Pantagruel*, nor the Egyptians' reaction to the slave, to depict
Rabelais's readers' reaction to this element of his first narrative.
(Rabelais took the Ptolemy anecdote almost verbatim from Lucian's
"To one who said 'You're a Promethius in words.'" As in Rabelais's re-
telling, so in Lucian's original there is no indication that the slave's
two colors refer to something specific in the author's work.)

On a more general plane, the study of the relationship between texts and their readers has become a major aspect of literary criticism and theory during the last two decades. Whereas the present study is concerned with the author's response to his readers' reactions to his texts, most reader-response critics and theorists concentrate upon the ways that a text shapes and structures the reader's reaction—or, in certain cases, the way that the reader shapes and structures (his/ her image of) the text. A good introduction to the work being done in this field can be obtained from two anthologies: *Reader-Response Criticism: From Formalism to Post-Structuralism*, ed. Jane P. Tompkins (Baltimore: Johns Hopkins University Press, 1980); *The Reader in the Text: Essays on Audience and Interpretation*, ed. Susan R. Suleiman and Inge Crosman (Princeton: Princeton University Press, 1980). Both have particularly good introductory essays on the history and development of this field of literary study.

30 This topic is developed much further in chapter 1 of Richard M. Berrong, *Every Man for Himself: Social Order and Its Dissolution in Rabelais*, Stanford French and Italian Studies (Saratoga, Calif.: Anma Libri, 1985).

31 Cohen uses the word "justice" for the French *raison*.

32 Rabelais's contemporary, Martin Luther, very definitely accused the masses involved in the Peasants' War of being in league with the devil. See Luther's "Against the Robbing and Murdering Hordes of Peasants" (1525), in *Luther: Selected Political Writings*, ed. J. M. Porter (Philadelphia: Fortress Press, 1974).

33 At this point Professor Defaux raised a very valid question: "What about Friar John? He is given to sexual impulses, yet he remains extremely strong, extremely powerful, extremely efficient, a very effective warrior." Though I remain convinced of the soundness of my basic argument here, I confess that I do not have a completely satisfying answer for Defaux's question. Friar John certainly does not occupy the locus of power and authority in *Gargantua* the way Panurge and Pantagruel do in *Pantagruel*, but it is nonetheless quite true that he makes a fine soldier and is a leader, not just a follower.

3. The *Third* and *Fourth Books:* Continuing the Exclusion

1 The change from the humor of "Alcofribas Nasier" to the humorlessness of "François Rabelais" actually occurred in two stages. The first (1546) title page read (in part): "Composed by M. Fran. Rabelais

doctor of Medicine and Priest [*Calloïer*] of the Hieres Islands." The Hieres Islands are off the coast of Provence in southern France; *calloïer* was a term used in the Orient. Sixteenth-century Frenchmen would have known that the Hieres Islands did not have a "calloïer" (the title would have struck them somewhat the way we would be struck today by "grand Llama of Staten Island"). As of the 1552 Michel Fezandat edition of the *Third Book*, however, Rabelais removes the comic second title, leaving only "Doctor of Medicine."

Natalie Zemon Davis has proposed a different but not incompatible explanation for the change from *Pantagruel* and *Gargantua* to the *Third* and *Fourth Books* regarding the absence or presence of a dedication. In "Beyond the Market: Books as Gifts in Sixteenth-Century France," *Transactions of the Royal Historical Society*, 5th ser., 33 (1983): 80–81, she explains that Renaissance Shepherd's Calendars, Books of Hours, collections of popular plays, farces, and songs, and the like were not published with dedications because they were seen as "texts which are so much common property, so much part of the *res publicae,* so much part of the currency of everyday discussion that no one has the right to appropriate them even long enough for a gift." This observation leads Professor Davis to suggest that Rabelais may have published his first two narratives without dedications because "he wanted the stories he had authored to have this quality of common property." Given this perspective, one might argue that if Rabelais did affix dedications to the *Third* and *Fourth Books* it was as yet another way of indicating that these works were not to be seen as emanating from the common heritage of popular culture.

2 Was gout seen in the sixteenth century as a rich man's disease?

3 On the subject of excrement, there is perhaps a parallel to be noted between the *Third Book* and *Pantagruel*. In *Pantagruel*, Panurge has a debate with the English savant Thaumaste carried on solely with gestures. Part way through, "Thaumaste got up in great alarm, but as he did so let a great baker's fart—for the bran followed it—pissed very strong vinegar, and stank like all the devils. Upon which the spectators began to hold their noses, since he was shitting himself with anguish" (236; *P* 111). In the *Third Book*, Panurge also carries on a "conversation by gesture," this time because his interlocutor, Nazdecabre, is a deaf-mute (chap. 20). The narrator remarks that, at the beginning of the "conversation," Panurge "took a longish yawn, and as he yawned he made, outside his mouth, with the thumb of his right hand, the figure of the Greek letter known as *Tau*, which he

frequently repeated" (342; *TL* 145; my italics). As M. A. Screech has suggested, this mention of the Greek letter might have been intended, in part, as a reference to *Thau*maste and the similar scene in *Pantagruel*. If this justifies a comparison of the two, one might note that, while Nazdecabre also becomes very excited during his exchange of hand signs with Panurge, he, unlike Thaumaste, never loses control of his sphincter muscles.

4 Again, one could make something of a comparison with *Pantagruel* in a somewhat parallel instance. When the one survivor of the massacre of the 660 Dipsodians tells Pantagruel that Anarche's troops are accompanied by 150,000 prostitutes, Panurge, having promised to destroy the Dipsodian army, says that he is bothered by only one thing: "How I can manage to roger all those whores there this afternoon; 'so that there remains not one that I in common form don't drum.'" Pantagruel's reaction to Panurge's boast is simply a good-natured "Ha, ha ha!" (253; *P* 138).

5 Her parting gesture to Panurge and Epistemon would certainly seem to be a "popular" one: "On the doorstep she hitched up her gown, petticoat, and smock to her armpits, and showed them her arse" (335; *TL* 132).

6 On the general European attitude toward witches in the fifteenth and sixteenth centuries and the sudden increase in their persecution at this time, I refer the reader to the second chapter of H. C. Erik Midelfort's fascinating *Witch Hunting in Southwestern Germany* (Stanford: Stanford University Press, 1972).

7 Along the same lines, one might note that it is Epistemon (and not Pantagruel) who recommends that Panurge consult the astrologer Her Trippa (356; *TL* 176). Even though there is no question of Her Trippa being a male witch, his strange, occult ways of seeing (or claiming to see) into the future may have made him too risky a figure to associate with Pantagruel.

8 Michel Beaujour, *Le jeu de Rabelais* (Paris: L'Herne, 1969), 25. Beaujour's reaction to this change is a sad one. For him, the "truth [of *Gargantua* and *Pantagruel*] is in the popular discourse that draws everything into a whirlpool in which hierarchies disappear" (p. 87). If the *Third Book* does not have such a "truth"—i.e., if it is not concerned, in Beaujour's eyes, with an undoing of establishment values ("No new aspect of learning is called into question after *Pantagruel* and *Gargantua*" [25])—the work is of no interest to him. Though Bakhtin dismissed from his consideration important passages in the

narratives (like the description of the Abbey of Theleme) because he did not regard them to be typical of "the true" (i.e., his) Rabelais, at least he never discarded entire narratives.

9 Jean Paris, *Rabelais au futur* (Paris: Seuil, 1970), and Henri Lefebvre, *Rabelais* (Paris: Editeurs Français Réunis, 1955). I might feel some compunction about using these critics as straw men to advance my own arguments if they did not so often delight in categorically (and ungraciously) dismissing their scholarly predecessors (and, often, betters). The Golden Rule has its negative side as well.

10 As anyone familiar with Lucien Goldmann's masterful study of Racine and Pascal, *Le Dieu caché* (1956; translated as *The Hidden God*, 1964), will readily perceive, Paris's formulation of Lefebvre's analysis owes as much to Goldmann as to Lefebvre, just as Beaujour's Bakhtin owes as much to the writings of Georges Bataille as to Bakhtin. (I have yet to discover where Julia Kristeva's presentation of Bakhtin comes from. Certainly not from Bakhtin.)

11 For a very solid and extremely entertaining discussion of this issue, cf. J. H. Hexter, "The Myth of the Middle Class in Tudor England," in *Reappraisals in History* (London: Longmans, 1961), 71–116.

12 See Paris, *Rabelais au futur*, chap. 4 (pp. 178ff.).

13 The original French text is included in a collection of Mauss's writings entitled *Sociologie et anthropologie* (Paris: Presses Universitaires de France, 1966). For an English translation, see Marcel Mauss, *The Gift: Forms and Functions of Exchange in Archaic Societies*, trans. I. Cunnison (New York: Norton, 1967).

14 Contained in Georges Bataille, *La Part maudite* (Paris: Editions de Minuit, 1967).

15 Michèle Richman Pollack, "Goods, Words, and Women: Georges Bataille's Theory of General Economy" (Ph.D. diss., Stanford University, 1974), 16. See also her expansion of this study: Michèle Richman, *Reading Georges Bataille: Beyond the Gift* (Baltimore: Johns Hopkins University Press, 1982).

16 In summarizing Paris's argument, I have actually organized it somewhat more clearly than Paris did himself. Because he does not distinguish between the Panurge of chapter 2 (who is arguing in favor of uncontrolled, unrecuperable spending) and the Panurge of chapters 3–4 (who is defending lending and borrowing, and hence a closed, recuperative system of exchange), Paris's analysis becomes rather confused. (It also becomes particularly weak when he tries to introduce Marx's distinction between a system of exchange based on

goods valued for their possible use and a system of exchange based on money valued for its potential for purchase [182–84]. Though, in chapters 3–4, Panurge certainly sings the praises of a general system of perpetual exchange, constant lending and borrowing, he is using his verbal cleverness to justify—and distract people from—his own actions, which involve only borrowing, and hence no reciprocity. As a result, and despite Paris, he is no more an example of Marx's system of exchange based on goods for their possible use than is Pantagruel. Neither wants continual, reciprocal exchange.)

If I might be allowed a personal reflection, Paris's analysis is symptomatic of the major problem with both his and Beaujour's works. The authors are so intent on making use of various theories and theoreticians fashionable among "New Critics" that they end up producing interpretations which, however appealing to the New-Critical establishment, have no real relation to what is going on in Rabelais's text.

17 Cf., for example, Marvin Harris, *The Rise of Anthropological Theory* (New York: Thomas Y. Crowell, 1968), 486–87.

18 As already mentioned, Beaujour does avoid the pitfall of applying Bataille to the opening chapters of the *Third Book*. In fact, he describes the Panurge of the third narrative as "a bourgeois recently won over to bourgeois values" (116), or, a few pages earlier, "a man of the people changed into a warden" (109). "Recently won over" is still highly questionable, however. The Panurge of *Pantagruel*, so well described and analyzed by Gérard Defaux in *Pantagruel et les sophistes* and *Le Curieux, le glorieux, et la sagesse du monde*, is hardly "un homme du peuple."

19 On *why* Panurge insists upon being disorderly in the face of Pantagruel's general imposition of order, see chap. 2 of my *Every Man for Himself: Social Order and Its Dissolution in Rabelais*, Stanford French and Italian Studies (Saratoga, Calif.: Anma Libri, 1985).

20 In the Prologue to the fragment of the *Fourth Book* published in 1548, the narrator addressed himself to *goutteurs très precieux* ("most dear tipplers") (*QL* 286). The 1548 Prologue is not included in Cohen's translation. For an English version, see *The Works of François Rabelais*, ed. Albert J. Nock and Catherine R. Wilson (New York: Harcourt, Brace, 1931), 2:933–38.

21 Cf. *Le Disciple de Pantagruel: Les Navigations de Panurge*, ed. Guy Demerson and Christiane Lauvergnat-Gagnière (Paris: Nizet, 1982), chaps. 18–28.

22 An important personage had not been portrayed in so undignified an action since *Pantagruel,* when Pantagruel tried to imitate Panurge's "fart, leap, and a whistle" (255; *P* 143).

23 One might also note that when Rabelais adapted the character of Bringuenarilles from *Les Navigations de Panurge,* he left out the scene in which the giant, having fallen asleep on one bank of a river, has an erection of such magnitude that "his member . . . stretched out to the other shore across the water, and stayed that way the whole night." See *Le Disciple de Pantagruel,* chap. 4.

24 On the other hand, the narration does not repeat from *Les Navigations de Panurge,* from which Rabelais borrowed Bringuenarilles, the scenes where the giant propels his boat by farting into the sail, or where he almost drowns a carter, his horses, and his cart in his urine. Neither does the *Fourth Book* make use of the story about the island where all the inhabitants have "the cleanest arses in the world" because they are required to join them together as a dyke to keep the sea from flooding their land. See *Le Disciple de Pantagruel,* chaps. 4 and 29.

25 Bakhtin often says that "in Rabelais' novel . . . fear is destroyed at its very origin and everything is turned into gaiety. It is the most fearless book in world literature" (B 39, 90, etc.). Could he really have remembered the *Fourth Book* when he wrote this?

On the emphasis in the *Fourth Book* upon participation in the defense of society, see chapter 3 of my *Every Man for Himself.*

26 This preoccupation in the *Fourth Book* with the material to the exclusion of the metaphysical has already been pointed out by Michel Jeanneret, in "Les Paroles dégelées (Rabelais, *Quart Livre,* 48–65)," *Littérature* 17 (1975): 14–30. I have difficulty agreeing with Jeanneret when he argues that Rabelais equates this materialism with a view of language as monovalent (whereas Pantagruel, Jeanneret maintains, does not share his crew's materialism and displays an appreciation of language's polyvalence). From there, Jeanneret asserts that the closing chapters of the *Fourth Book* are, at least in part, an allegory, or lesson, in reading the Rabelaisian text. Rabelais's readers must learn not to reduce or restrict the text to any one meaning; rather, they must learn to perceive and appreciate its potential polyvalence.

Though I find Jeanneret's opening pages to be sound, I am not convinced by his argument that the others on board the *Thalamege* (other than Panurge) are particularly more materialistic than their captain, or that their perception of the possibilities of language is really all that different from his.

PART III

1 A knowledge of popular culture in the twentieth century would not have been sufficient here. Bakhtin himself argued that Carnival ceased to be carnivalistic as of the second half of the eighteenth century (*Dos* 131), so one could not extrapolate back from twentieth-century popular culture to reconstruct its sixteenth-century equivalent.

2 Stanley E. Fish, "Interpreting the *Variorium*," in *Reader-Response Criticism: From Formalism to Post-Structuralism*, ed. Jane P. Thompkins (Baltimore: Johns Hopkins University Press, 1980), 164–84.

3 Julia Kristeva, "Bakhtine, le mot, le dialogue et le roman," *Critique* 23 (April 1967): 438–65.

4 The standard work on the Franciscan influence in Rabelais's work is Alban J. Krailsheimer's *Rabelais and the Franciscans* (Oxford: Clarendon Press, 1963).

5 Cf. for example: "What brand of justice is it that any nobleman whatsoever or goldsmith-banker or moneylender or, in fact, anyone else from among those who either do no work at all or whose work is of a kind not very essential to the commonwealth, should attain a life of luxury and grandeur on the basis of his idleness or his nonessential work? In the meantime, the common laborer, the carter, the carpenter, and the farmer perform work so hard and continuous that beasts of burden could scarcely endure it and work so essential that no commonwealth could last even one year without it. Yet they earn such scanty fare and lead such a miserable life that the condition of beasts of burden might seem far preferable" (*Utopia* 238–39).

6 Lefranc's essay on *Gargantua* has been reprinted in Albel Lefranc, *Rabelais* (Paris: Albin Michel, 1953).

7 One could adduce other reasons for Rabelais's abandoning of *Utopia*, largely related to the shift in economic mentalities from *Pantagruel* to *Gargantua*. For a study of this shift, see Richard M. Berrong, "The Evolving Attitude toward Material Wealth in Rabelais's *Oeuvres*," *Stanford French Review* 9, no. 3 (Fall 1985). The exclusion of *Utopia* is another factor making *Gargantua and Pantagruel* less "popular" as of the second book.

ADDENDA

P. 127, n. 1   *La Cultura popular* . . . , trans. Julio Forcat and Cesar Conroy; *L'Opera di Rabelais* . . . , trans. Mili Romano; *Literatur und Karnival* . . . , trans. Alexander Kämpfe. There also appear to have been translations in Polish (Krakow, 1975), Czech (Prague, 1975), and, although I could find no printed reference to it, Rumanian.

P. 140, n. 6   Jean Dupèbe has just recently uncovered more evidence regarding the date of Rabelais's death, which has led him to alter his original hypothesis. See Jean Dupèbe, "La Date de la mort de Rabelais (suite)," *Etudes Rabelaisiennes* 18 (1985): 175–76.

P. 148, n. 14   "La Notion de dépense" has just become available in English as "The Notion of Expenditure," pp. 116–29 in Georges Bataille, *Visions of Excess: Selected Writings, 1927–1939,* ed. Allan Stoekl, Theory and History of Literature, 14 (Minneapolis: University of Minnesota Press, 1985).

P. 151, n. 3   Kristeva's essay is available in English as "Word, Dialogue, and Novel," pp. 64–91 in Julia Kristeva, *Desire in Language: A Semiotic Approach to Literature and Art,* ed. Leon S. Roudiez (New York: Columbia University Press, 1980).

More generally, I should mention that Early Modern European historians interested in popular culture and its reception by the establishment are now evidently talking less in terms of Burke's "exclusion" than of changing relationships. This was the one point that Natalie Zemon Davis emphasized when we discussed my work this summer (at a lunch kindly arranged by Thomas P. Roche, Jr.). Since then several Early Modern European historians have recommended David Warren Sabean's *Power in the Blood: Popular Culture and Village Discourse in Early Modern Germany* (Cambridge: Cambridge University Press, 1984) as a particularly outstanding example of this perspective.

Index